Keep Faith Growing:

it matters more than church growing

Philip Campion

GILEAD
BOOKS
PUBLISHING

First published in Great Britain, February 2018

www.GileadBooksPublishing.com

2 4 6 8 10 9 7 5 3 1

Copyright © Philip Campion 2018

British Library Cataloguing-in-Publication Data:

A catalogue record for this book is available from the British Library.

ISBN: 978-1-9997224-3-2

Cover design: Nathan Ward

Contents

Introduction

The pictures on the seed packets look brilliant! There is an abundance of perfectly formed unblemished flowers, a crop of greenfly-free sun-ripened fruit, cabbages without a hint of caterpillar damage, all grown from tiny seeds. Anyone who has ever planted some seeds, and watched them germinate, become seedlings, develop into plants, and then produce their own fruit and seeds, will know how remarkable this process is. But they will also know that the growth from seed to flower and flower to fruit is nowhere near as easy as the pictures on the packets suggest!

When it comes to our spiritual lives, the same can also be true. We have a seed: it is called "the Word of God", and for Christians that is the Good News of Jesus, God's son, who brings us life, joy, peace and hope. But what is that seed going to grow into? What is the picture on the packet? And can it really be that easy to grow?

As someone who has been a Christian Minister for more than four decades, I look back with a measure of alarm that we have got the picture on the packet faith wrapped up in a box, neatly stored for emergency use, but mostly to sit there, just in case.

Costly faith is recognising that Jesus is Lord, which means he is the one to whom we owe allegiance, loyalty and above all love. To believe in Jesus is to relinquish the right to rule our own lives, and to seek his rule, his control over everything we are, everything we say and everything we do. John speaks about the consequence of believing in Jesus as having *"life in his name."* We could translate that as *"living under his authority"*, which also describes the Kingdom of God. And remember that the Kingdom of God was described by Jesus as a seed which grows!

Religion and Faith

If we think like this then we begin to realise that faith has very little to do with religion. James writes at the end of his letter in the New Testament, *"Religion that God our Father accepts as pure and faultless is this: to look after orphans and widows in their distress and to keep oneself from being polluted by the world"* (James 1:27). 'Religion' in most people's minds is the performance of ritual. That may be fairly obvious in terms of set liturgies, ceremonies, the reciting of prayers, the singing of psalms and hymns etc., but it is equally applicable to the more informal gatherings of church with contemporary music and prayer. These rituals specifically acknowledge we belong to the community of Christians: it is a way of underlining the faith that we have as Christians, and it can be part of the way in which our faith grows. But it is not in itself what faith is about. When James speaks of religion he speaks of how we respond to the needs of other people, and how our lives are different from the lives of those whose focus is not God, but the world. This is the faith which lives life under Jesus' rule. Religion, as men practice it, is established by set form and pattern, but the faith John speaks about is organic, living, and also growing. *"Our hope is that, as your faith continues to grow, our sphere of activity among you will greatly expand"* (2 Corinthians 10:15). Religion doesn't grow, but true faith does.

Bear Grylls is widely known as a man of adventure and challenge. He is currently the Chief Scout. A recent documentary has him spending time in the Alaskan wilderness with the former President of the United States, Barak Obama. Clearly the programme was heavily stage managed, but nonetheless there was a genuine chemistry between the two men, which led to the final question from Bear to the President, *"can I pray for you?"*, and a simple prayer was spoken there and then in the wilderness, by just a very down-to-earth human being, for another ordinary human being, who happened to be President of one of the most powerful nations. Faith here had nothing to do with religion but everything to do with living. In his book *"Mud sweat and tears"*, Bear Grylls wrote of his own faith: *"As a kid, I had always found that a faith in God was so natural. It was a simple comfort to me: unquestioning and personal".*[5] But then he describes how he was forced to *"sit through somewhere in the region of nine hundred dry, Latin-liturgical, chapel services"* at the boarding school where he was sent for his education.[6] There was a disconnection between his inner sense of faith, and the religion he was being shown. That set up a confusion in his mind which was resolved only some years into his school life when a crisis hit him (one of many in his subsequently rather risk riddled life) and he cried out *"Please God comfort me".* Bear writes, *"Blow me down...He did".*[7]

[5] Grylls, B. (2011). *Mud, Sweat and Tears.* Transworld Publishers, London. pages 112-114. Used with permission under fair use guidelines of Penguin Random House
[6] Ibid.
[7] Ibid.

From that experience Bear grew a strong personal confidence in the Christian Faith: *"The more of the Christian faith I discover, the more I realise that, at heart, it is simple...Faith in Christ has been the great empowering presence in my life, helping me walk strong when so often I feel weak".*[8] The words *"empowering presence"* bring to mind a book by Gordon Fee called *"God's Empowering Presence: the Holy Spirit in the letters of Paul"*. The thesis of this book is that Paul understood the work of the Holy Spirit to be utterly essential to being a Christian. Fee wrote in the book: *"For Paul Christian life not only begins by means of the Spirit; the whole of Christian life is a matter of Spirit. In the kingdom of God not only righteousness but also peace and joy are effected by the Spirit* (Rom. 14:17)".*[9] The Holy Spirit is the "Comforter" (a translation of a Greek word for Holy Spirit John uses in his Gospel.). Bear Grylls first real prayer was *"Comfort me"* and the response in his life was of course the work of the Comforter, the Holy Spirit. The Holy Spirit is the presence of God in us who

[8] Ibid.
[9] Fee, G. (1994). *God's Empowering Presence*. Baker Publishing. Permission granted under fair use.

empowers us to have the sort of faith that is genuine, and accompanies us in every situation.

Bear Grylls speaks of this faith, this empowering presence of God in his life, "*helping me walk strong when so often I feel weak*". Paul wrote of his own experience, "*But he (the Lord) said to me, 'My grace is sufficient for you, for my power is made perfect in weakness.' Therefore I will boast all the more gladly about my weaknesses, so that Christ's power may rest on me. That is why, for Christ's sake, I delight in weaknesses, in insults, in hardships, in persecutions, in difficulties. For when I am weak, then I am strong*" (2 Corinthians 12:9-10). If you know anything about Bear Grylls, then you would hardly think of him as weak. He is one of these crazily fit, healthy, athletic types with a dogged determination that has led him to be accepted into the SAS, climb Mount Everest and conquer many other gruelling physical challenges. [10] Yet he knows that he is genuinely a frail human being who recognises his need for a higher power, a stronger authority and a source of life greater than his own. And that he has found in God, in his faith in the empowering presence of Christ.

[10] Special Air Service, the Special Forces unit of the British Army

This is the faith God gives us in the "Word", the Good News about Jesus. This is the faith I believe is to keep growing in us. In the following chapters I want to consider the three most vital aspects for healthy growing in faith. The first is conversation, the way we listen to and talk with God. I want to explore, from the years I have been part of this Christian adventure, the key place of the Bible and prayer in our lives. The second is curiosity, the way we continue to explore the Word of God and apply its wisdom to the realities of our lives. I want to share with you some of the ways I have been, and continue to be, curious about the Gospel, about children and faith, about science, about suffering and about our own personal development. The third is connection, the balance we need to find between our personal faith in the Lord, and our coming together as believers into the church that declares his goodness to our world. Connecting to God is vital, but he wants us to connect with each other and connect to the world.

Some words of Jesus seem to capture what is the purpose of these chapters. He said, *"Ask and it will be given to you; seek and you will find; knock and the door will be opened to you"* (Matthew 7:7). Asking is about entering into a conversation with God, seeking is about being curious to find out more of God, and knocking is about our intention to make connections, with God and then with others.

There have been some special moments of growth in my life, special discoveries of God's grace which I hope will be an encouragement to you, both to grow your faith and to give yourself to the growth of others. Let me give you one of those now.

Whilst at Bible College I befriended a Romanian Pastor called Joseph Ton. He had come to the college to do a theology degree, but without the permission of the Romanian Authority, which at that time was a communist regime led by Nicolai Ceausescu. We both left college in 1972, Josef returned to Romania and I started my work as a church leader. In 1980 I decided to take my wife and two children on a camping trip through Europe to visit Joseph. Little did I know then that the trip would start a relationship with the Christians in Romania which has taken me back there almost every year since. I reckon I have spent more than a year of my life there in trips over 36 years! That first trip opened my eyes in two ways. First, I saw the hand of God in our comings and goings, where we experienced the first of many miracles as we journeyed and visited the believers. We arrived at

Joseph's house one Saturday afternoon, astonishing Joseph, who told us, "How did you know we were here? We only came home last night and are going away again on Monday". We had not planned that: God had. We ended up taking Joseph with us around the country and were introduced to others who have been our friends ever since. Joseph was forced out of his country two weeks after our visit. The timing of everything was perfect, but then it was God's plan not ours.

My eyes were also opened by seeing the faith of the believers who were under huge pressure from communism at that time. One of things that struck us was the contrast between life in the streets of Romania and life in the church context. Outside was dark and dreary and people walked with faces downcast; inside was light with smiling faces and a genuine sense of warmth.

The connections I have with Romania have been so precious and I am very grateful to Joseph, to Petru (who died some years ago), to Eugen, to Sorin and many others for their encouragement to me as I have sought to share something of God's grace with the Christians in that country.

On a very recent trip to Romania I spent a week with a group of young families, at a Christian holiday centre in the Western Carpathian Mountains. Each morning I spoke with them about the importance of keeping their faith growing. I recounted the time a friend and I were stopped by the Securitate – the Romanian Secret Police—from taking an internal flight to Timisoara for a Good Friday evening meeting, but were allowed on the late flight that same evening. Walking through the almost pitch black streets of the city, trying to remember the way to our friend's house, we noticed a lady in front of us who I thought might be the pastor's wife. We quickened our pace and she turned round to see who was following her and burst out into a smile and a greeting "Philiiiip" (the second "i" in my name always gets lengthened by the Romanians!). She said how anxious they had been about us, and took us home immediately, to be plied with typical Romanian hospitality. The faith of the believers in the country affected me—they were living in a hostile environment, and yet refused to disown Jesus.

At the end of the holiday with the young families, they shared their encouragements from the week. One man spoke movingly about how he felt his faith had become stagnant, but was now determined to see it grow once more. He then said that at first he was resistant to my message because he thought I was saying that church did not matter; only faith mattered. But after the week he realised that if his faith grew and the faith of them all, then church would change. I had said nothing all week about the church changing; only about their faith growing, however he had come to see that if our faith grows, there will automatically be growth and change in church.

So we will begin our exploration of the three aspects of keeping faith growing; conversation, curiosity and connections. All of this will lead us to reconsider the picture on the seed packet! It will have to be a faith picture, because it is faith we are called to grow. John makes this so clear when he writes, *"Dear friends, now we are children of God, and what we will be has not yet been made known. But we know that when Christ appears we shall be like him for we shall see him as he is"* (I John 3:2).

So let's get into the asking, the seeking and knocking, and as we do so let faith grow!

Chapter 1

Conversation

Living faith can grow through conversation. You may be more familiar with the idea of prayer but, as I hope to explain, conversation is so much richer than what we often mean by prayer. Living faith implies not just the existence of God, but the possibility of conversation with God. The Bible starts and ends with conversations. In Genesis chapter 1 God speaks into being the whole of creation, and then in chapter 2 God speaks to the man he has made. In chapter 3 God calls out to Adam, *"where are you?"* and the conversation follows. Note it is God who begins the conversation (Genesis 2:16;3:9). The last book of the Bible begins with a conversation between John and the risen Lord Jesus. Again the conversation is begun by Jesus who says to John, *"do not be afraid"* (Revelation 1:17). The final words of the Revelation contain another conversation between the Lord and John or maybe his people: *"Yes, I am coming soon."* And the reply is, *"Amen. Come, Lord Jesus"* (Revelation 21:20).

As we explore the rest of the Bible we can conversations between God and his people. Abraham talks with God about God's promise to him to be the father of a great nation, asking Him: *"What can you give me since I remain childless?"* (Genesis 15:2). Moses talks with God out in the wilderness (Exodus 3v4), and continues to do so throughout his life. This summary of Moses' relationship with God is so revealing: *"The Lord would speak to Moses face to face, as one speaks to a friend"* (Exodus 33:11). The boy Samuel sleeping in the temple under the care of the old priest Eli, initially thought it was Eli talking to him when he heard someone call him one evening, but Eli knew better. He knew that God wanted to talk with his people and he understood that God wanted to converse with Samuel, even though he himself seemed to have lost the art of God-conversation (1 Samuel 3:1-4). In all these stories God begins the conversation. In the book of Samuel it is said by the story writer that *"In those days the word of the Lord was rare"* (I Samuel 3:1). The Message paraphrase of the Bible puts it like this: *"This was at a time when the revelation of God was rarely heard or seen"* (MSG). Was it rare for God to speak, initiate conversation, or for the people to hear God, and respond to God? Is it in the nature of God to keep silent for years on end? If we are to engage in conversation with God we need to understand that God still wants a conversation with us, and we need to be much more aware of his voice.

An old hymn begins; *"What a friend we have in Jesus, all our sins and grief to bear, what a privilege to carry everything to God in prayer"*.[11] The emphasis of this is our talking to God, however there is little in the poem to suggest a conversation with God. Indeed the only hope of God's response is in the line, *"In his arms he'll take and shield thee, thou wilt find a solace there"*. I can think of times in my life when the conversation with God has been much like this: I pour out my heartfelt worries and cares to Him, and I am deeply comforted by believing that he has heard and has taken me and my concerns into his great big arms of love. But conversation really does suggest both parties speaking. I want to believe that the writer of the tune to which we used to sing *"What a friend we have in Jesus"* understood this and therefore called that tune *"Converse"*. I discovered that it is called *"Converse"* because the man who wrote it was called Charles C Converse. Converse is an Old French name which came to England and hence America; one of the

[11] Scriven, J. M. (1855). *What a Friend We Have in Jesus.*

American Converse family members founded a shoe factory which produced the All Star converse trainer! Whether Charles C Converse knew that the hymn he was accompanying was about conversation with God or not is of no importance. What matters is that we realise just how much God wants to be in conversation with us.

The writer to the Hebrews puts it like this: *"Long ago, at many times and in many ways, God spoke to our fathers by the prophets, but in these last days he has spoken to us by his Son, whom he appointed the heir of all things, through whom also he created the world"* (Hebrews 1:1-2).

God spoke in many ways. Whichever the ways God used, and still uses, we receive his speech through our understanding of words. I may see something beautiful in creation, and think to myself, "thank you Lord for this sign of your goodness and love." The word from God is "This is a sign of my love to you" and we respond with our heartfelt appreciation. It may not have been a spoken word initially but God is speaking through this, and his word is personal to us.

So as we explore the art of conversation with God, let's first consider how God speaks to us, under the heading of "the Word of God", and then consider how we speak to God under the heading of "Prayer".

The Word of God

We tend to use the phrase "the Word of God" without thinking what it really means. We use it for the Bible, we use it for Jesus Himself, and we use it for the Gospel message, but we can all too easily neglect the simplest use of "word", as something which is spoken. *"Can I have a word please?"* means *"I want to talk with you!"*—ever since God came looking for Adam in the Garden of Eden His cry to us has been, *"can I have a word?"*; Hebrews tells us that *"God has spoken to us"*.

When Paul told Timothy to *"preach the word"* (2 Timothy 4:2), he uses the term "logos." That is the term which John uses in his gospel to begin his account of Jesus coming to live among us. *"In the beginning was the Word, and the Word was with God, and the Word was God...the Word become flesh and made his dwelling among us"* (John 1:1, 14). The better way to translate "preach the word" is "tell people clearly about Jesus". That is why one reason Alpha is such an effective tool, it sets out to explain clearly who Jesus is, why he died and why following him today is possible. But this explanation alone cannot make the seed of faith to germinate and grow. People need to hear God speaking to them. They do not only need to hear the message about Jesus but they need to hear Jesus speak to them.

In Romans chapter 10 Paul links faith to hearing the Word. He says simply that people will not come to faith unless they hear the Good News. He sums up his thinking like this: "*So faith comes from hearing, and hearing through the word of Christ*" (Romans 10:17). I have used a different Bible version here because it makes very clear the two stage process about which Paul is talking. First, he says that people hear of Jesus as someone shares the message with them, and then he says they hear Jesus speaking to them. He says they hear *"through the word of Christ"*. The first stage is someone preaching, or just talking about Jesus, and then the second stage is the listener hearing, not just the preaching or the story telling, but "hearing" in a deeper way. They hear the Word as if God were speaking just to them. Many people will say that when they heard the message about Jesus at an Alpha course, in a sermon, or in a personal testimony, it is as if God is speaking directly to them; they hear the speaker with their ears, but in their heart they hear God. There is a tendency to think that it is our preaching which leads people to faith, whereas Paul says that it is God's word spoken to them which leads them to faith. They need to hear God speak. They need to realise God is beginning a conversation with them!

I was excited to have a text message very recently from a friend of mine whose wife is not yet committed to being a disciple of Jesus, but has been asking questions; wondering, looking, and above all noticing the changes in her husband as his faith has grown. The text message simply said, *"Hey Phil, M felt God speaking to her on Sunday."* When people begin to realise God has a word for them and wants to converse with them, then faith has truly begun to grow.

John the fisherman follower of Jesus wrote to his friends: *"That which was from the beginning, which we have heard, which we have seen with our eyes, which we have looked at and our hands have touched – this we proclaim concerning the Word of life. The life appeared; we have seen it and testify to it, and we proclaim to you the eternal life, which was with the Father and has appeared to us"* (1 John 1:1-2). He tells them that what he and the others have been talking about is from God. It is God's word to them and for them, and it came in the person of Jesus. John continues, *"I write to you, young men, because you are strong, and the word of God lives in you, and you have overcome the evil one"* (1 John 2:14). What John says he and the other witnesses of Jesus have done is to tell the believers clearly about Jesus. Then the word they have heard has gone inside them, it has become personal to them. Instead of being something to be received with their minds, it has become someone to be received with their hearts, an invitation not from John or Paul or Peter, but from God himself.

The idea of a "word" living in us needs thinking about. Consider how many words we hear which do not become alive in us. We can listen to someone speak, but the words, as we say, "go over our heads," or, "in one ear and out of the other." The same goes for words we may read, whether in a book or on some form of internet media. They mean nothing more than a car that flashes past us as we stand on the pavement. But then, unexpectedly, we hear or read a word which, like a car out of control, mounts the pavement and crashes into us. The word sticks, lodges in our hearts and then continues to affect us. A negative comment about our behaviour or our looks, a judgement against us, can become a word which has been personally addressed to us, which we have taken in and believed, and then by which we are controlled. Much pastoral care involves helping people question and deal with negative words which have lodged in their lives from the past.

But in the same way a negative word can car crash our lives, so a positive and good word can lodge in our hearts. Someone might speak an affirmation, or an encouragement, and we really believe what they are saying—that is more like a bus stopping at the pavement and inviting us on board. And it takes us forward in our lives.

Sadly it seems that we are far more likely to have negative words lodge inside us than positive ones. It has often been said (though this is by no means a tested truth, just a generalisation), that it takes ten positive words to counteract the effect of one negative word on a person.

The Bible warns us of the consequence of negative words, *"The words of the reckless pierce like swords, but the tongue of the wise brings healing"* (Proverbs 12:18). But it also encourages us to take on board the words of God: *"Then he taught me, and he said to me, 'Take hold of my words with all your heart; keep my commands, and you will live"* (Proverbs 4:4). Psalm

119 is a special song, celebrating the word of God. It uses different ways to describe this word, law, precepts, commands, statutes, decrees, but they are all used to suggest that the word of God is something so crucial to life, so vital to everyday choices, so significant for dealing with life's challenges, that we dare not cease to listen to it: *"Your word is a lamp for my feet, a light on my path."* (Psalm 119:105), *"Your statutes are always righteous; give me understanding that I may live."* (Psalm 119:144). We need God's word inside us. We need to hear it, but, more than that, we need to understand this is God speaking into our lives so that they are directed in the way that pleases him. And for this reason we need to give very careful attention to how this word of God lives in us.

At the start of John's letter he writes about the word we hear from God, and affirms its authenticity. This is the word *"from the beginning."* It is God's word, and it has power to affect us if we choose to receive it. There is life in the word of God because it comes from the breath of God. We only speak words when we breathe out through our voice box, and God's word is similarly breathed out by His Spirit with the life and power of God in it.

When Jesus came and began speaking, the people were amazed. Luke tells us that one day Jesus went to the religious meeting place in his hometown of Nazareth and, as was the custom, offered to read the Old Testament Scriptures. He read a passage from Isaiah which spoke about someone coming who would heal people, set them free and give them new life. When he had finished reading he sat down and everyone was looking at him. The way he read words which the people had heard before was different; the words had power. Jesus began to talk more and tell them that the very thing Isaiah had promised was now happening. He told them that he himself is the one sent by God to give life. Luke then tells us the people were even more affected by what he said: "*All spoke well of him and were amazed at the gracious words that came from his lips*" (Luke 4:22).

The words that Jesus spoke came with the breath of God—that is why they had such power and such grace. The breath of God is another way of describing the Spirit of God. Jesus, filled with the Spirit of God, spoke words from the mind of the Father through the breath of the Spirit: God's words, Spirit inspired words, life changing words.

Somehow we need to allow the word of God, the spoken invitation through Jesus, to come to people in a way that is God speaking to them, and not us preaching to them. We need to believe that it can and will lodge in their hearts.

So what does this mean in practice? Let me first talk a little about the Bible and then about the prophetic word.

a.   The Bible

Chris Duffet is an evangelist, who loves telling people about Jesus. He has lived in a small village in Cambridgeshire for over five years now and slowly people have got to know him. A man in his 50's became sick with cancer and his wife asked Chris to call. Chris did and shared the gospel with the man before he died. His wife then asked Chris to take his funeral. Chris had never taken a funeral before, so he asked me to help and I met the man's family with Chris and we talked about their grief and about the funeral. When the time came for the service I was asked to read the Bible. The church was packed with lots of villagers who wouldn't normally be seen in church, and I read Jesus words: *"Do not let your hearts be troubled. You believe in God; believe also in me. My Father's house has many rooms"* (John 14:1).

Something happened as I read: people listened with attentiveness: "what is this? These words have power." It wasn't my power in reading them, it was the power of the Spirit at work as they were read. The Spirit of God was bringing the truth into the lives of those who were listening: *"Do not let your hearts be troubled." "Comfort, comfort my people says your God."* (John 14:1, Isaiah 40:1)

It is my conviction that when words like these are read out loud today, just as when Jesus first spoke them, the breath of God is being poured out. We have sometimes underestimated the power of Scripture. Perhaps we have turned the words into texts: to be put on posters or added to Christmas cards, when really they need to be spoken.

When Jesus was in the wilderness after his baptism, Matthew records that after fasting for forty days he was hungry. The devil tempted him to use his power as the Son of God to turn stones into bread. Jesus' reply was, *"It is written, 'Man shall not live on bread alone, but on every word that comes from the mouth of God'"* (Matthew 4:4). We need to realise that when we read Scripture we are becoming the mouthpiece of God. Reading the Bible has to be more than just an exercise, whether that happens on our own, or in the context of "church" (any gathering of the believing followers of Jesus), or indeed among those who do not yet believe.

But here we have a problem; perhaps one we have not really faced! Is what I am saying true for all the Bible? What about the difficult parts? What about the long lists of rules in the book of Leviticus, or the lists of names in the first book of Chronicles, or the accounts of mass killing in the books of Kings, or the obscure words about other nations in some of the Old Testament prophetic writings? Or what about the book of Revelation in the New Testament? I think there are two things we can say about this which I hope will help.

Firstly, every part of the Bible has something of God's life to share with us. *"All Scripture is God-breathed and is useful for teaching, rebuking, correcting and training in righteousness"* (2 Timothy 3:16). That is exciting. When I read a lengthy part of, say, 1 Chronicles chapter 2, I read lists of names that I can hardly pronounce: *"Caleb's concubine Maakah was the mother of Sheber and Tirhanah. She also gave birth to Shaaph the father of Madmannah and to Sheva the father of Makbenah and Gibea. Caleb's daughter was Aksah"* (1 Chronicles 2:48-49). How can that be a word of God?

Let me suggest that if I am open to God I might hear him say as I read these names, "These are all people of my family, just as the people in that list of names in your church directory on the table over there. Everyone one of them matters to me." I may hear God say, "I know some of these people seem to have a strange background (the idea of concubines goes against the biblical concept of marriage), but they all matter to me whatever their background." Likewise, I can hear God speaking through the whole "story" of the people of Israel throughout the accounts of their history in the Old Testament. As they turned away from God and God called them rebellious, I can either say, "well, that explains what happened to that group of so called 'Christians'", and name my favourite gone off track church or Christian leader, or I can hear God saying, "you have rebelled as well, yes you, I'm talking to you."

Now this sort of listening to the Bible is something we need to encourage far more, and we do so by example, by making sure that we listen as we read the Bible, even to the hard parts! I don't like the accounts of killings in the Old Testament, but as I tell God that, I can hear him saying, "Do you think I like that? I most certainly do not, but the people had to discover that I am the Lord, the Sovereign over all the nations. But hear this too, that I am full of mercy and my mercy extends way beyond the borders of those who thought I was only their God. I love the world and as you read on you will discover just how great that love is, great enough to send my One and Only Son into the world to bring the world back to me." *"All Scripture is God-breathed and is useful..."* is the truth.

Secondly, when I read to others words spoken directly by Jesus, or by the prophets who spoke directly from the heart of God, I need to read and listen as if these words are being spoken right now into my life, by God, just like when I read Jesus' words in John 14 to the mourners at the funeral service.

As I hear the Bible read on Sundays, I find myself increasingly disappointed with the response. Have we heard God speak? Too often our reply is no, we haven't because we haven't preached, or listened to preaching, yet. But that suggests our interpretation of the words, our explanation, is more important than the word itself. If we can believe that the words spoken from God, which we read out loud, are being spoken by the Spirit into people's lives, then we should believe that the words on their own have power to reach into people's hearts. Then we may just read them a little more slowly, carefully, deliberately, lovingly and expectantly.

Recently there was a British programme which documented the earliest television programmes for children. One which had huge popularity, and was still being broadcast when my own children were small, was "*Jackanory*". It was simply someone reading a story! But before the days of television, and when I was a toddler, there was a radio programme called "*Listen with Mother*". Again, it was simply someone reading a story, but in such a way that it felt like they were talking just to me! "Listen with Mother" had a catch phrase at the beginning of each episode: "*Are you sitting comfortably? Then I'll begin.*" I wonder if we shouldn't make more of reading the Bible, especially when it is the gospel words, or a prophetic passage. "Are you sitting comfortably?" hardly sounds appropriate for hard wooden pews. But maybe we should say "Are you sitting expectantly? Are you ready to hear God?" When I first went to Romania, I was surprised when everyone stood for the Bible reading. Now perhaps I can understand that they were saying how important these words are. But sadly, I did not sense that the congregation responded any more to the words, because they were standing up! Indeed if the passage was too long they fidgeted, and as soon as the passage ended they sat down! I would rather we had comfortable chairs so I could say, "are you sitting comfortably? Then I'll begin!"

One of my own guiding principles comes from a verse in Isaiah which I discovered years ago and have treasured ever since: *"The Sovereign Lord has given me a well-instructed tongue, to know the word that sustains the weary. He wakens me morning by morning, wakens my ear to listen like one being instructed"* (Isaiah 50:4).It is as if God says, *"Can I have a word with you?"*

b.   The prophetic word

In the past the subject of prophecy has led to a great deal of controversy in the church, both in the United Kingdom and elsewhere. It relates to whether or not the gifts of the Holy Spirit are understood as being only for the first Christians in New Testament times, or for all the followers of Jesus for all time.

I remember how as a young Christian growing up in a church where the gifts of the Holy Spirit were not believed to be part of the Christian life, I began attending a youth meeting (we called them "squashes" because for the most part they took place in someone's front room which meant we were squashed into the small space available), and heard the idea that the gifts were for today. I went to the leader of my church, a godly Baptist Minister called Samuel Nash, and asked his advice on the matter. He said very little to me, but gave me two pamphlets. One explained why the gifts of the Holy Spirit ceased to operate after the New Testament age, and the other explained how one could, as a Christian, be filled with the Holy Spirit and discover his gifts today. He did not tell which was right, but gave me the opportunity to explore myself, to read the Bible and discover what God had to say to me. My journey of discovering more of the Holy Spirit began then and continues to this day.

That word "more" gained popularity in the days of what was called the Toronto Blessing: simply asking God to pour out more of his Spirit on us. A theologian called Simon Ponsonby wrote a book some years after that time called *"More"*. It was subtitled *"How You Can Have More of the Spirit When You Already Have Everything in Christ."* He writes, *"The desire for more of*

God is a sign of spiritual health. The mature want more".[12]

That is a vital understanding for all of us. And it leads to an issue that has been part of my whole ministry. Simon quotes the words of Billy Graham, the highly respected American Evangelist: *"Billy Graham once wrote, 'everywhere I go I find that God's people lack something. They are hungry for something. Their Christian experience is not all that they expected and they often have recurring defeat in their lives. Christians today are hungry for spiritual fulfilment. The most desperate need of the nation today is that men and women who profess Jesus be filled with the Holy Spirit'".*[13] This is part of the growth in faith which I long for all of us, and it calls for a curiosity of spirit which to me is a vital part of growing faith. We will consider the issue of curiosity later.

But back in my early days of faith I was curious about the gifts of the Spirit and, as the years have gone by, with so much of the church embracing the gifts and exploring the part they play in our lives, I have been drawn back to what Paul wrote to the church in

[12] Ponsonby, S. (2004). *More*. David C Cook, Used with permission.
[13] Ibid.

Corinth: *"Follow the way of love and eagerly desire gifts of the Spirit, especially prophecy. For anyone who speaks in a tongue does not speak to people but to God. Indeed, no one understands them; they utter mysteries by the Spirit. But the one who prophesies speaks to people for their strengthening, encouraging and comfort. Anyone who speaks in a tongue edifies themselves, but the one who prophesies edifies the church"* (1 Corinthians 14:1-4).

The prophetic word is given to Christians, both to encourage and grow the faith of fellow believers and to bring a sense of God's word to those who, as yet, are still unbelievers. It is simply God's Spirit speaking through us as we witness for Jesus. If we think of the prophetic word as only for a chosen few, like the prophets of the Old Testament, we are avoiding the truth that Jesus promised his Holy Spirit to all of us. Paul urged us to receive him and to *"eagerly desire gifts of the Spirit especially prophecy."* But if we believe the Holy Spirit brings a prophetic word into our lives, then we can begin to develop the conversation we have with the Lord, based not just on our speech but on his message to us.

We have thought about the Word of God as the words of the Bible, spoken as God's words to us today. I believe we need also to be open to the prophetic word, God speaking to us in all sorts of contexts. Let me try to describe some of them.

1. We can start with the reading of Scripture as we have already considered. I do believe that, just as in one sense all Scripture is God breathed and therefore is God's voice to us, there will be words which we hear as if God is saying them to us right then and there. The verse or passage becomes a prophetic word for us at that moment. I listened recently to a testimony from a couple who have been through a deep, dark challenge. The husband, a very fit and active man, was diagnosed with cancer which required very swift intervention, surgery, and chemo- and radiotherapy. At the darkest point he was in hospital with severe pneumonia, on a drip and breathing oxygen, and his wife was at home crying and trying to pray. She said, "I am not one to play lucky dip with my Bible, but I opened it and it was Psalm 41: *'Blessed are those who have regard for the weak; the Lord delivers them in times of trouble. The Lord protects and preserves them – they are counted among the blessed in the land – he does not give them over*

to the desire of their foes. The Lord sustains them on their sick-bed and restores them from their bed of illness'" (Psalm 41v1-3). Those words came to her as if God was speaking, just there and then. And she trusted the Lord, and believed her husband would recover. There is a difference between reading a verse because it says what we want to hear and hearing Scripture knowing God is speaking right there and then to us. It is about having this conversation with God, and believing he has something to say to us.

2. As we preach or sit and listen to a sermon, we should be listening for the prophetic. What is it in the words that is conveying God's message into our lives? Into this church? Or into this one person? I believe we need to help those who are beginning to develop the gift of speaking, whether that be with Sunday messages, in home groups or wherever, to expect that God will speak through them and that they are to become more aware of this happening. This, for me, is the point of the letter to the Corinthians in which Paul says, *"When you come together, each of you has a hymn, or a word of instruction,*

a revelation, a tongue or an interpretation" (1 Corinthians 14:26). Paul is assuming that people contribute, but what they contribute needs to be a word from God not just their own ideas. We have read into this passage warnings against disorder and forgotten that the underlying assumption is that God will speak through the people: there will be prophetic input. So, as we speak, we must be aware of this possibility and indeed seek it.

3.   As we pray corporately we should expect the prophetic. It has been a longing of mine to encourage this sort of praying when we are together. So many people believe they cannot take part in corporate prayer; their fear rules over any possibility of them speaking out loud. Often people think of corporate prayer as asking God to intervene in this world issue or that personal concern and the more eloquently we can do that the better, so most people consider their prayers not good enough. But if we think of prayer as a conversation between God and his children, we can all contribute, however childlike we may feel our prayer is. Jesus encouraged us to think of ourselves as receiving

the kingdom of God *"like a child"* (Mark 10:15). So then, as we pray and bring our concerns to God, very simply, without telling God what to do, we should expect God to speak to us. Often God does speak through the prayer someone offers, and yet we miss the moment, or pass by it all too quickly. In Romans chapter 8 the Holy Spirit is said to help us in our weakness, in the matter of praying. As someone prays, there are times when it sounds like a personal rant against this or that pet hate, such as the godless state of our nation. Or it can sound like the checklist of needs that must be prayed for all in one go; all those who are sick, all those who are homeless, all those who are broken etc. But there are other times when someone hesitantly brings a concern to God, confesses they really don't know what to pray but longs for the grace of God to meet the need, and you sense God is speaking: "My grace is sufficient. It really is, please trust me in this. Do not be anxious any more, it is in my hands now." In all this, remember we are growing our conviction that God is in the business of conversation.

4. As we pray on our own we can hear the prophetic. Paul tells how he suffered from a particular niggle in his life; he called it a thorn in the flesh. He prayed about it, and God replied: *"Three times I pleaded with the Lord to take it away from me. But he said, 'My grace is sufficient for you, for my power is made perfect in weakness'"* (2 Corinthians 12:8-9). Let me continue the story of the sick man and his wife by telling you the man's experience. He was feeling as low as possible and utterly helpless, even to the point where he had to have surgical nappies. He cried to God that he felt just like his very young granddaughter. And then, as if from nowhere, he knew God was speaking to him: "You are like your little granddaughter. And what does she do? She looks to her father, your son, who puts his arms out wide, and she runs to him and throws herself into his arms. Listen, my Son the Lord Jesus is waiting for you, his arms are open, just throw yourself into his arms, and you will be safe". The man said those words were a complete revelation to him, and changed his attitude almost instantly.

5.   As we go about our daily lives we should expect
      God to speak through what we see and what we
      hear. As I am out and about I will sometimes say
      to my wife, "look at that poster" or, "did you see
      that flower that is like...?", and what follows is
      an illustration of something God is saying to us.
      But this isn't just about sermon illustrations, it
      is about hearing God speak to us. As Jesus
      walked around, the things he saw became
      illustrations of things His Father was saying:
      "Look at the birds of the air" (Matthew 6:26),
      "See how the flowers of the field grow" (Matthew
      6:28), *"The kingdom of heaven is like a net that
      was let down into the lake and caught all kinds of
      fish"* (Matthew 13:47), *"Seeing a fig-tree by the
      road."* (Matthew 21:19). If we believe that God is
      the Creator, then the Earth and everything
      around us is his creation. We should see his
      signature on all of it: not just the natural
      wonders—though personally I will never tire of
      looking at the world of nature—but also the
      creativity of others. For me, the combination of
      the two, natural beauty and human creativity,
      speaks volumes of God's love. A powerful
      example is the work of a New Zealander called
      Belinda   Simpson,   who   uses   her   own

photography of butterflies and the words of various writers to produce inspirational books titled *"When butterflies speak"*. A quotation such as, *"We delight in the beauty of the butterfly yet rarely admit the changes it has gone though to achieve that beauty"*, together with a magnificent Monarch butterfly, has the power to open our minds to God's word: about the challenges we are facing, and how he is at work changing us through those difficulties. [14]

6. As we speak to those who do not know Jesus, we should be attentive to the prophetic. This is one of the most exciting aspects of growing faith in our conversation with God: as we speak with others, and they share something of their lives with us, we can hear God telling us words to say which will bless them. And blessing is far more powerful than we realise. *"Blessing is God's presence on the move"*, as one of my college tutors once said to us: it is the power of God released through our words into the lives of others. It can be healing, encouraging,

---

[14] Simpson, B. (2012). *When Butterflies Speak*. Xlibris Corporation. Permission requested

challenging, mind opening, and faith building, but if it is from God it will have effect. So, as we talk with people, we need to learn to listen for the word which will bring life from God to them.

God desires to have his full part in our conversation. He speaks through His Word the Bible and through the prophetic word given by the Spirit through his people. That's his part: now let's think a little more of our part, which is what we usually call prayer.

Prayer

I have often been pressured in my ministry by well-meaning church members to have more prayer meetings. I would say that this has been consistent in all the places I have been: "If the church had a better attended prayer meeting it would grow! If we had more nights of prayer we would see more blessing. The church just does not pray enough!"

Throughout the past four decades many books have been written and read on the subject of prayer. If you put the subject of prayer into the online Christian bookstore *www.eden.co.uk*, you will be told they supply 2897 products on this topic! All the well-known Christian authors have written their own book or books on prayer. I have read a good few and been genuinely encouraged in my praying by most of them.

At the same time there have been many prayer initiatives taken to urge the church to be more prayerful. I remember my first "night of prayer" was held in Bedford as a joint initiative by the churches in the large cold Anglican building of St Paul's. There had been calls for weeks of prayer, and then weeks of prayer with fasting. I remember how this swept up some of my colleagues into what seemed almost a competition to see who could pray and fast the most. I am quite sure they had no intention of being competitive, and I am also sure they were significant times. But I have had a worry in the back of my mind that somehow we have missed the point.

If we allow ourselves to think that God responds in proportion to the quantity and fervency of prayer, we are in danger of entering the arena where things happen in the Christian life because of what we do, rather than by the grace of God. And that is why I believe Jesus told us: *"And when you pray, do not be like the hypocrites, for they love to pray standing in the synagogues and on the street corners to be seen by others. Truly I tell you, they have received their reward in full. But when you pray, go into your room, close the door and pray to your Father, who is unseen. Then your Father, who sees what is done in secret, will reward you"* (Matthew 6:5-6). So, for me, as much as I have wanted to encourage the church to pray, and indeed hosted prayer meetings of many different types, my greatest concern is to develop people's conversation with God, so that they might grow in their faith.

As a child I was told that the shortest verse in the Bible (and therefore the easiest to remember) was *"Jesus wept"* (John 11:35). But there are two other verses which in English consist also of only two words. They are: *"Rejoice always"* and *"Pray continually"* (1 Thessalonians 5:16 and 17). I wonder why these get less attention than John 11:35? *"Rejoice always"* is about an attitude of mind and heart that keeps enjoying God's grace and goodness even though sometimes in the world there is little or nothing to rejoice about. John 11 tells us that Jesus wept over the death of Lazarus, and shared in the pain of Lazarus's sisters Mary and Martha. So *"rejoice always"* doesn't mean "never be sad"; but it does mean keep in mind there is joy in knowing Jesus! We could expand that, but our attention needs to come back to prayer, and to the next phrase from 1 Thessalonians 5, *"pray continually."* In the same way that *"rejoice always"* doesn't mean never be sad, *"pray continually"* doesn't mean never do anything else but pray. This is not about becoming a monk and sitting in a little cell spending all our hours in the physical action of prayer. But it is about an attitude that keeps in mind the presence of God and our freedom to converse with Him at all times and in all places. It is about making prayer far more of an everyday part of life and far less of a religious exercise. That is what I believe Jesus wants us to discover and grow into.

The story of Jesus raising Lazarus from the dead in John 11 illustrates this well. Jesus arrived at the home of his friends Mary and Martha, and found them grieving over the death of their brother Lazarus. They were both upset with Jesus because they thought that if he had come sooner he could have healed Lazarus. But Jesus had deliberately waited; he knew what was going to happen. He went with the sisters to the tomb where the body of Lazarus had been placed and asked that the stone be taken away. Then we read, *"Jesus looked up and said, 'Father I thank you that you have heard me. I knew that you always hear me, but I said this for the benefit of the people standing here, that they may believe that you sent me'"* (John 11:41-42). Jesus spoke as if he had been in conversation with the

Father over this matter already, and now was simply letting the people know that he and the Father were doing this together! They had been talking about Lazarus, and now Jesus was going to call Lazarus alive out of the tomb. The conversation had been going on all the time.

Among all the books on prayer on the Eden website, I discovered one by Rosalind Rinker which like many others is simply called *Prayer* but which has as a subtitle, *Conversing with God*. Her summary is that prayer is a dialogue between two persons who love each other.[15]

Jesus spent whole nights conversing with his father. I believe that conversation is the key to prayer and one of the keys to growing faith. Jesus followed the words about praying *"to your Father who is unseen"* by sharing the words which we call the Lord's Prayer. The context of the prayer given in Matthew is the believer in her or his own room, having a conversation with God (Matthew 6:6), but we have taken it into the context of a formal gathering of believers reciting words together. Luke records the

---

[15] Rinker, R. (1986). *Prayer: Conversing with God*. Zondervan

words of the Lord's Prayer after a request from the disciples: *"Lord teach us to pray, just as John taught his disciples"* (Luke11:1). But then Jesus follows the words with the story of a man who calls on his friend at midnight asking for some bread. The context is friend to friend, one to one.

One book which did have a real impact on me was by the Canadian author Jeremy Sinnott; it's called *"Audience of One"*, a title used in varying forms by others as well.[16] This book came out of the renewal movement which began in the 1980's and has been ongoing ever since with the rediscovery of the practice of spiritual gifts. As we have noted earlier, this movement has all too often polarised Christians, we tend to be either very much in favour of these gifts or very wary of them. But I believe that if we hold to the principle that prayer is conversation with God, then we will find a way to steer though the obstacles that the issue of spiritual gifts may put in our way.

In 1 Corinthians 14, where Paul calls us to *"eagerly desire gifts of the Spirit, especially prophecy"* (1 Corinthians 14:1), he goes on to say, *"for anyone who*

---

[16] Sinnott, J. (1999). *Audience of One.* Destiny Image Publishers

speaks in a tongue does not speak to people but to God. Indeed, no one understands them; they utter mysteries by the Spirit" (1 Corinthians 14:2). Speaking in tongues is part of one's personal conversation with God. It is not something for sharing, with the specific exception of a message which has a clear, understandable interpretation. The gift of speaking in tongues can be such an asset in one's own conversation with God, as long as we remember that it is firstly a gift, and not a cause of thinking we are somehow better than anyone else, and, secondly, that it is part of a conversation and we need to be quiet and listen as well as speak.

My first real exploration of this gift came when I had been in ministry for about eight years. And I was worn out! Monica and I had two sons, and we had decided to get involved in foster care. One of our foster children came to us with an undiagnosed mild case of Hepatitis. I caught the virus and became seriously unwell. A friend of ours, John Taylor, was staying with us whilst training for the Ministry at the Northern Baptist College. He arrived one evening when the illness was at its most critical point and the doctor was preparing to admit me to hospital. John knelt by my bed and prayed for me. I have no recollection of the prayer, but a strong recollection of a battle through the night which subsided early in the morning. When the doctor came around 8.00am, he took one look at me and said, "You've turned the corner, I think you can stay at home." I recovered, but it took a couple of months and when I returned to my church I felt completely empty and unable to serve. I had been preaching and leading in my own strength and now that strength had gone I had nothing left to give. At the same time I connected with a group of ministers hungry for more of God. I began to meet with them, often up in the Lake District, at Hawkshead Chapel. And there my own spiritual hunger grew, and a longing for more in my relationship with God. One morning as they prayed for me, I was aware of God in a fresh and invigorating way, a way that put me on the floor, (quite literally) but enabled me to stand again in something of God's strength. I found that came from and with speaking to God in words, not of my language, but "speaking in tongues." It was a means to express wonder in God and a longing for God that seemed to lift my spirit and focus my mind more on God's love than on my own issues, whatever they were.

From that came a desire to again share with my church the grace and love of Jesus, but in a fresh way. We asked several visitors to come and help us, and one who stands out in my mind was a local Anglican Bishop who ever so gently invited the Holy Spirit to come. As with other churches it wasn't an easy time and I am sure I made mistakes in communicating what God was doing. But I observed that where there was a hunger for God, recognising that we can do nothing without Him, but that with Him all things are possible, there was a growth in faith—a growth in the conversation of prayer and a discovery of spiritual gifts.

This gift of speaking in tongues was an issue in the early church and no doubt it will continue to be an issue. But for me there are two fundamental principles I want to hold to. The first is that speaking in tongues is a precious gift of the Father by the Spirit to his children to help them in their conversation with him. The second is that if it is ever spoken of or thought of as a token of favour, if it is ever worn as a badge of superiority, or if it is ever used as a reason for judgement, then it ceases to be a blessing. Blessings are good so let's make sure we keep this one so.

Prayer is part of the faith-growing life God wants us to experience. I long to help people to pray more, but really I think a lot of our formal praying has not helped. Jesus words need to be heard again, *"But when you pray, go into your room, close the door and pray to your Father, who is unseen. Then your Father, who sees what is done in secret, will reward you"* (Matthew 6:6). That word 'reward' sounds good doesn't it? Eugene Peterson in the Message paraphrases this verse: *"Here's what I want you to do: Find a quiet, secluded place so you won't be tempted to role-play before God. Just be there as simply and honestly as you can manage. The focus will shift from you to God, and you will begin to sense his grace"* (MSG). The reward God gives is always his grace. He gives himself, and in himself are the riches of his kindness, his mercy, his attention, his comfort, his strength. When we have a deep conversation with someone we know that something of ourselves has been given to them, and we have received something of the other person. That's what God wants for us all the time.

There is a place for what we think of as prayer, asking God for His help: *"I urge then, first of all, that petitions, prayers, intercession and thanksgiving be made for all people – for kings and all those in authority, that we may live peaceful and quiet lives in all godliness and holiness"* (1 Timothy 2:1-2). It is good to note that the context of prayer is the environment in which we live and work, and the content of prayer is both asking and thanking.

When it comes to the more personal matters of our lives, James writes in his letter, *"Is any among you in trouble? Let them pray... Is anyone among you ill? Let them call the elders of the church to pray over them and anoint them with oil in the name of the Lord. And the prayer offered in faith will make the ill person well"* (James 5:13-15). The subject of prayer and healing is again one that has caused many to be wary, unsure whether the healing power of God is to affect us here and now or in the new bodies God has promised us after we die. Equally, we might think that the power to heal lies in our praying rather than in God's grace. Given those understandable concerns, it remains part of the mandate of the followers of Jesus to pray for healing.

I want to encourage all of us as followers of Jesus to do this whenever we come across any form of sickness in any person. It should be as natural as any feeling of sympathy or concern, a desire to bring this need for healing to Jesus, and it should be persistent!

In Luke's gospel we read, *"Then Jesus told his disciples a parable to show them that they should always pray and not give up"* (Luke 18:1). His story contrasts the persistence of a widow with the indifference of a judge. The widow, ill-treated by someone, keeps coming to the local magistrate to seek justice. The judge initially refuses her petition but eventually gives in, not because he cares about justice but because he doesn't want to keep being bothered by the widow! Jesus' point is that, if this careless judge gives in to the preserving plea of the widow, how much more will God, who is a good judge, respond to the persevering prayers of his people? The story ends with these words: *"I tell you, he will see that they get justice, and quickly. However, when the Son of Man comes, will he find faith on the earth?"* (Luke 18:8). One of my strongest convictions is that God will see justice is done; it is so important for people who have been treated so unjustly in their lives. Justice may not come quickly enough for us, but Jesus assures us it will come, and quickly in the bigger scheme of things. So we are to keep praying, and not to give up. And this perseverance itself is a sign of faith, as Jesus made so clear at the end of the story.

When I quoted the above verses from James chapter 1, I omitted a phrase from verse 13, *"Is anyone happy? Let them sing songs of praise"*. It is as if James is saying, "whatever your situation, engage in the conversation with the Lord". I believe that if we see prayer in this way, whether it is crying to God out of pain or praising God out of gratitude, we will want to listen and discover what God has to say to us in that situation. And his word has the power of life.

Some words which have been with me from my days as a young believer come from a poem written by an Indian Christian, Narayan Vaman Tilak, back in the early 1900's.

> *Prayer to a heart of lowly love, opens the gate of heaven above.*
> *Ah, prayer is God's high dwelling-place, wherein His children see His face.*
> *From earth to heaven we build a stair, the name by which we call it, prayer.*
> *Prayer is the gracious Father's knee; on it the child climbs lovingly.*

*Love's rain, the Spirit's holy ray, and tears of joy
are theirs who pray.*[17]

Kicking leaves

Much of what I have just written has come out of
years of seeking to grow in faith. Another key moment
in that process came when I realised that the
challenge of ministry is all-consuming. By this I mean
that there were so many tasks each day that I was
spending not enough time listening. Thankfully some
wise elders were able to help me see this, and gave me
the courage to change. One of them said to me, "you
need to take time to kick leaves". It was as if a whole
new world opened up to me! I remembered how as a
child I loved kicking leaves when we walked in the
autumn woods. So I began to take time out just to
walk and that grew into time to talk with God, and
time to listen. I realised the importance of this for
everything else I did and the need for it to be a central
part of all that I did. Walking and talking was not
leisure on my "day off", but an intentional part of my
working life, to allow my soul time to breathe and give
my mind time to converse with God. Now I have
retired from leading church I have much more time to

[17] Tilak, N. V. (1862-1919) *Prayer to a heart of lowly love.*

give to this, and realise even more its creative power. I continue to be saddened by stories of church leaders who have become exhausted by the work of ministry, often because of the impossible demands and expectations church puts on them, and because of their own inability to stand back and take time out.

One of the books that influenced me many years ago and remains a nagging reminder in my spirit is *"The practice of the presence of God"* by Brother Lawrence. It is hardly a book, more a series of letters and interviews written by a 17th Century Carmelite monk. In it he says *"that we should establish ourselves in a sense of God's Presence, by continually conversing with Him. That it was a shameful thing to quit His conversation, to think of trifles and fooleries."* He speaks of the contrast between the set prayers of his religious order and this continual conversation with God: *"I have quitted all forms of devotion and set prayers but those to which my state obliges me. And I make it my business only to persevere in His holy presence wherein I keep myself by a simple attention, and a general fond regard to God which I may call an actual presence of God; or, to speak better, an habitual, silent and secret conversation of the soul with God, which often causes me joys and raptures inwardly, and sometimes also outwardly, so great that I am forced to use means to moderate them, and prevent their appearance to others".[18]*

Another book that has inspired me to grow my conversation with God has been a little volume, mostly of quotations by other Christian authors, compiled by Tommy Tenny called *"The Heart of a God Chaser".[19]* Many of the words in that book remind me that there has to be a deliberate intent on our part to engage with God in this conversation. It doesn't just happen. Of course here is one of great paradoxes of all I am trying to say. As a child and a teenager and even beyond I was encouraged and indeed commanded to have a quiet time: to set aside time each day to read the bible and pray. This has to be an excellent idea! The problem with it arises when it becomes a set duty and loses the excitement of conversation which can be continued throughout the day. I want to help young Christians discover this constant conversation with God, and have found this happens far more naturally with them than I realised. A teacher who had recently

[18] Lawrence, B. (1693). *The Practice of the Presence of God.* Wilder Publications 2008
[19] Tenny, T. (2000). *The Heart of a God Chaser.* Albury, Struik Christian Books

become a Christian talked to me about how he found himself praying as he drove to school in the morning, during the lesson when the kids were becoming difficult and even at lunch time in the staff room. He is learning and growing the art of conversation with God. Tremendous!

John says in his letter, *"you are strong because the word of God lives in you"* (1 John 2:14). These words have come with fresh power to me recently. It is so easy to think John meant that if we "read, learn and inwardly digest" the Bible, then we will be strong. But there is more to it than that. John is suggesting that we can have an on-going conversation with God. His "word", i.e. God speaking to us, is part of our life. Our strength, our growth in faith, comes from this conversation, the most amazing reality for everyday living.

One final comment about this. The more we grow in faith, the more we will realise how great our God is. We will see that, though God invites us into conversation and indeed calls us to pray continually, the partnership is far from equal! The power is all God's. One of my favourite illustrations of this comes from a book on prayer by a writer called Dutch Sheets: *"It sort of reminds me of the mouse and elephant who were best friends. They hung out together all the time, the mouse riding on the elephant's back. One day they crossed a wooden bridge, causing it to bow, creak, and sway under their combined weight. After they were across, the mouse, impressed over their ability to make such an impact, said to the elephant, "we sure shook up that bridge, didn't we?"[20]*

[20] Sheets, D. (1996). *Intercessory Prayer.* , Baker Publishing. Used with permission

Chapter 2

Curiosity

There's an anecdote often told at the start of the Alpha course, which goes like this: a father and his son went fishing one day. After a while in the boat, the young boy began to ask his father some questions, "Dad, this boat is made of steel. How come it floats?" The father thought for a moment, and said, "I'm not sure son." After a little while, the boy asked, "Dad, how do fish breathe underwater?" The father thought for a while and said, "That's a good question son, I'm not sure." Once more the boy asked his father, "Dad, why is the sky blue?" Again, the father thought for a while and replied. "I'm sorry son, I don't know. I think I used to know once but I guess I forgot." Worried that he was annoying his father, the boy said, "Dad, do you mind my asking you all of these questions?" "Of course not son", his father said... "If you don't ask questions, how will you ever learn anything?" I can relate both to that boy and to that father! I love asking questions and finding out things I do not know.

Imagine I am walking along the beach in South Wales, the sea stretching into the misty horizon on one side and the cliffs rising up steeply from the sand on the other, and I notice movement at the top of the cliff face. A bird, seeming to float in the air, dives down to the ground before lifting off again and flying away at great speed—what is it? Too big for a kestrel, wrong shape for a kite, it has to be peregrine falcon! But I also know the frustration of not knowing the answers, questions not just about birds and butterflies (I can search for information about them on Google!), but about why things happen to people, and what is going to be the outcome for them.

In his book *"Encounters with Jesus"*, Tim Keller writes about the young girl Mary, who was engaged to marry the carpenter Joseph, and how she reacted when the angel told her she was going to become pregnant, not by the normal method of sexual union, but by the divine intervention of the Holy Spirit. Keller remarks how we often see Mary's response in terms of her shock and then her submission. Of course she is blown away by the very idea of having a child this way, and that the child is supposed to be the Son of God, yet, as we know, she accepts it with grace: *"I am the Lord's servant, Mary answered. May your word to me be fulfilled"* (Luke 1:38). But Keller goes on to say we all too easily miss another reaction, that of doubt, of honest questioning, of curiosity. Mary asks the angel, *"How can this be?"* (Luke 1:34) and Keller comments that without Mary's doubt, her curiosity and questioning, we would never have had the statement from the angel which is so powerful, *'nothing will be impossible with God.'* (Luke 1:37)".[21]

Nicodemus was a highly educated man, and a member of the religious leadership of Jesus' day. Yet he was curious to know more about Jesus. He came to see Jesus at night: presumably because he was concerned about some of his fellow leaders who disapproved of Jesus and probably also disapproved of asking questions! Having expressed something of his questioning mind to Jesus, Jesus said to him, *"very truly I tell you, no one can see the kingdom of God unless they are born again"* (John 3:3). Now there's a statement that demands another question! How on earth can someone be born again? It's physically impossible! When this idea of "born again" has been used by Christians either to describe themselves, "I

---

[21] Keller, T. (2013). *Encounters with Jesus: Unexpected Answers to Life's Biggest Questions.* Hodder & Stoughton, page 199.

am a born again Christian", or to share faith with others, "You must be born again", they should remember that when Jesus first spoke those words, Nicodemus had questions about it; the idea of being born again needs exploration! And of course Jesus went on to give an explanation to Nicodemus. He was saying that, just as our first birth is into the physical world as a child of our parents, so we need to be born spiritually as a child of God. Nicodemus' questions led to another great lesson from Jesus: *"For God so loved the world that he gave his one and only Son, that whoever believes in him shall not perish but have eternal life"* (John 3:16).

I believe that asking questions, being curious, especially when it comes to our faith and to the ways God deals with us, is a very important part of keeping our faith growing. At the end of a section describing the wonder, beauty and dependability of God's love, Paul writes: *"For now we see only a reflection as in a mirror; then we shall see face to face. Now I know only in part; then I shall know fully, even as I am fully known"* (1 Corinthians 13:12). I have often wondered what Paul means by these words. The phrase "reflection as in a mirror" is actually quite unhelpful. When we look into a mirror we see a pretty exact likeness of our face—not always a pleasant sight! But in the days of the first century AD, mirrors were made of beaten metal, not glass, and the reflection they offered was far from exact. The word Paul uses for "reflection" is actually the word from which our word "enigma" comes. Paul says we look in a mirror and see a strange sight, a distorted image, more like the old hall of mirrors on the seaside pier! So in its context Paul is saying that, although we have this perfect ideal of love, when it comes to our experience of it we only see a distorted picture of love. However, he says there will come a day when love will be complete and we will fully understand the love of God. Commenting on this verse, Krish Kandiah in an excellent book called *"Paradoxology"* says: *"The paradoxes of our faith will not be resolved by this book, or any other book. They can only be explained – indeed, they will be fulfilled – when Christ himself comes again and all things are resolved in him. But in the meantime, it is good and proper for us, far from papering over the cracks, as we have done too often in so many different ways, to keep straining to see through that dark glass, in the hope we may discern clues and comfort from a loving God whose ways are often inscrutable to us".* [22]

If we are curious enough to ask God, to seek answers, to express doubts and to explore what is going on, then we may just find ourselves on the receiving end of a revelation that is enough to change our lives. I believe that curiosity is at the heart of faith which grows. When Jesus said, *"Ask and it will be given to you; seek and you will find; knock and the door will be opened to you"* (Matthew 7:7), I do not think he intended to limit this invitation to our initial discovery of him as our Lord. That would be like saying that once we have made that discovery there is nothing more to find out about Jesus. But he has more for us. We do not need to stop seeking just because we have found Jesus.

Curiosity goes hand in hand with childlikeness and it is highly significant that Jesus said, *"Truly I tell you, anyone who will not receive the kingdom of God like a little child will never enter it"* (Mark 10:15). In his much loved children's story *"Alice's Adventures in*

[22] Kandiah, Krish. (2014 UK Edition). *Paradoxology*. Hodder & Stoughton, Page 307. Used by permission of InterVarsity Press, P.O. Box 1400, Downers Grove, IL 60515, USA. www.ivpress.com

Wonderland", Lewis Carroll describes what happened when Alice ate the piece of cake in the glass box marked "Eat me": *"'Curiouser and curiouser!' cried Alice (she was so much surprised, that for the moment she quite forgot how to speak good English); 'now I'm opening out like the largest telescope that ever was! Good-bye, feet!' (for when she looked down at her feet, they seemed to be almost out of sight, they were getting so far off)".*[23] I have always been curious, though perhaps not to the extent of Alice!

I am sure childhood influences have played a part in my own eagerness to ask, to experiment, and to discover. I recall two experiences which probably had a large part in leading me to become a minister: the first was a children's group held on Sunday mornings at the church of which my family was a part, Leigh Road Baptist Church, in Leigh on Sea. The group was called "Children's' Own" and was run by a wonderful, generous hearted lady called Miss Tattersall. Her way of running the group was to let us run it! It was "our" meeting and she encouraged us to take full part in it. I remember how we asked a lot of questions and were

---

[23] Carroll, L. (2014). *Alice's Adventures in Wonderland.* Macmillan, Page 58

always encouraged to seek the answers for ourselves. The second experience was the Scripture Union Beach Mission held in our town: it was called a CSSM, which stands for Children's Special Service Mission, and it was led by an amazing couple of saints, David and Lynn Leech. They allowed me my first opportunity to share the Christian message in the open air. I remember as a teenager—it was 1966, the year England won the World Cup—leading one of the outdoor afternoon meetings in Chalkwell Park, Westcliff on sea. I had great fun inviting the children to take the free gift of fresh air, fill up their lungs and then sing their hearts out! But there was more to it than just a technique for getting a crowd of kids to participate; I wondered about what was going on in their lives as they sang songs about God and his love for them. I found myself being curious about how faith in Jesus really affected me and my life. I had to think about what I was saying to these children. I recall David Leech had a favourite song which we sang in the team meetings, "*Love never faileth, love is the way*". So many times I have brought the song to mind when facing tough situations with people, with whom there seemed to be no hope. I am still curious as to how God works in people's lives, bringing them to faith and then by His Spirit growing them in faith.

At school this curiosity was in full flow as I studied science in the Sixth form. I was fascinated with microscopes, which opened up the world of the miniscule. I always look back with gratitude to a Botany Teacher in my Sixth form, Mr Beattie, who made the exploration of the world of living cells so exciting that I wanted to find out more. It was nothing short of a revelation when I first prepared a slide of a section of plant stem, sliced finely with a razor blade, and was able to see complete xylem and phloem cells. That will probably mean little to you, but to me it was quite amazing. My curiosity continues to this day, especially into the new areas of exploration called Quantum Physics. But as my school days drew to an end I had a strong sense that God wanted me to train in Christian Ministry and, after completing my A Levels in science, I changed course and found myself studying theology at the Baptist Training College in Oxford, Regents Park. There I found tutors who encouraged my curiosity and helped me think and explore my Christian faith. The system of teaching to which I was exposed relied heavily on our personal efforts at digging into a subject, rather than on being fed with the material to be remembered for an exam. This served me well in keeping my curiosity thriving.

Curiosity, for me, is about realising that there is always more to discover about God and his ways. In fact, over my years in ministry I would say that what has kept me going is to continually find more to say, because God has said more to me. But this is not just for me! I am sure that God wants all his followers to keep growing in their faith by being curious, and "seeking" as Jesus said.

Let me look at some areas where I have been curious, that might both illustrate the importance of curiosity and make you think as well. Your areas may turn out to be quite different from mine, but what matters is that we all keep our minds open to see more of God as we grow in our faith.

Children and faith

Thinking back to my own childhood, I am reminded how much I owe to people like Miss Tattersall who, as I mentioned earlier, gave me the opportunity to explore my childhood faith. I have another hero in my mind from this era, a young Sunday school teacher called Paul Andrews. I can never tell him how much he inspired me; he died many years ago whilst in the prime of life. But his influence upon me was very significant. He told me and the others in our Sunday school class of his experiences in the army when he did National Service in the 1950's. What impressed me was his courage in standing up as a Christian in that context and being ready to defend his faith as well as his country. Faith was so significant to him that it was not a religious duty or a Sunday event, but an everyday confidence in God. And he was cool! And he played tennis very well!

As I think of those days in Sunday school, I have a strong sense that Paul and the other leaders accepted me and the other children as part of God's family. I do not recall being told constantly by them that I needed to repent and believe in Jesus. I do recall being affirmed as someone God loved. Over many years I have been involved in children's work in church, both in Sunday groups, which I much prefer to call something like "Kids Club" rather than "Sunday school", and in week long programmes for children such as Holiday Clubs and summer camps. I have always had a strong commitment to excellent children's work in our churches, but I have constantly been questioning what it is we are telling our children about faith and about their relationship with the Lord. I see our work with them as much more than teaching Bible stories; it is about engaging with children in the life of faith, praying with them, praising God with them, listening to the Spirit with them, and showing them how to be curious about the faith we have in Jesus.

For some years, together with my wife and a strong team of volunteers, I was involved in leading the Stoneleigh Bible Weeks organised by the Newfrontiers Network of churches. We had at its peak over 300 eight year olds for a week. I loved it, and I loved the reality of faith among these children. It also made me even more curious. These children, like myself as child, engaged with faith, and were part of its living, breathing reality. We sung with them, *"we are kingdom kids, kids of the kingdom, we let Jesus Christ be number one in our lives"*.[24] Yet to some adults, these children were not yet Christians, either because they hadn't yet "prayed the prayer" inviting Jesus into their lives, or they were not yet baptised. So were they Christians or not?

That led me to be really curious about what we think of children and faith. I read and researched and ended up teaching on the topic. The issue is that if we think

[24] Bailey, J. (1994). *We Are Kingdom Kids.* CD, https://jimbailey.bandcamp.com/album/kingdom-kids

that children move at a specific moment from not being a Christian to being a Christian, then we will want that to happen as soon as possible and so we will teach young children that they need to become a Christian. As very little children tend to do what grown-ups say, they will readily agree, and then logically we should open the door of faith to them in baptism and communion. That way of thinking is present in some churches where 4 and 5 year olds are baptised as believers.

Other churches will equally encourage children, however young, to become a Christian, but then tell them to wait to be baptised until they become an "adult" (and that can vary hugely in age!). Those churches may well welcome children to take communion as part of the believing family even though they consider them to be too young for baptism. They may also say to children that communion is only for those who are baptised, so, although they are considered Christians, they are excluded from communion.

Alongside this we have a large part of the Christian Church worldwide which practises infant baptism: baptising babies as a sign of their inclusion in God's family by grace and through the faith not of the baby but of their family and the church. Then, when the baby grows up and reaches an age of discernment (which again varies enormously from as young as 5 to 16 or over), they are confirmed as they consider this faith their own.

This issue is not just a theoretical debate among church leaders, but is relevant for all parents and all those who take part in work with children in a church context. Today that would include "Messy Church" along with holiday clubs, kid's midweek clubs, and Sunday meetings.

So what is Jesus saying to us? My curiosity has led me to two conclusions. The first is that Jesus welcomes children into his kingdom, simply because they are precious to him. If Jesus welcomes them, so should we. The story of Jesus taking children in his arms and blessing them is so powerful: as Jesus was talking, a group of "people" (Mark doesn't tell us whether they were dads or mums, but almost certainly they included mothers) brought some children to Jesus, with the purpose of getting His blessing for them. Let me quote what happened next, using the words of "The Message" paraphrase: *"The disciples shooed them off. But Jesus was irate and let them know it: 'Don't push these children away. Don't ever get between them and me. These children are at the very centre of life in the kingdom. Mark this: Unless you accept God's kingdom in the simplicity of a child, you'll never get in.' Then, gathering the children up in his arms, he laid his hands of blessing on them"* (Mark 10:13-16 MSG). The parents desired that Jesus might bless their children. Such a blessing given by a Rabbi was considered a sign of God's favour on the person being blessed. But as Jesus took them in his arms and blessed them I cannot see how you can avoid the conclusion that Jesus was including them. Far from *"shooing them off"*, Jesus was "letting them in".

This has led me to appreciate the importance of the "dedication" service which happens in some churches. It is like the Jewish practice of presentation which Joseph and Mary applied to their new son Jesus (Luke 2:22-24). But it is given fresh meaning for us when we believe in Jesus as the inaugurator of a new Kingdom. I believe as the church we need to make more of this dedication than maybe we have done. It is telling the world so clearly that this life is precious and significant to God. Children belong to the Lord. That leads me to trust that when a child's life ends, as does happen and will happen, I should not hesitation to talk of that child as safe in God's eternal care.

The second conclusion I have reached is that Jesus wants us to have a faith in him which is ours, chosen deliberately and relevant for the whole of our lives. There is no way that a little child can fully understand that, let alone agree to it. It has to be something which grows. This growing faith can start very early, so I love to invite the youngest children to be friends with Jesus, to understand his kindness, love, and his grace which forgives them (though the words we may use for this will be simpler, words about Jesus being sad when we are naughty but so pleased when we say we are sorry.) In our Stoneleigh meetings we had children who said they had become a Christian the previous year in the 7's (and the year before that when they were in the 6's!), but now in the 8's they want to ask Jesus again into their lives. Each "yes" to Jesus builds on previous "yeses" and strengthens the faith within that little life. As it grows, so the sense of belonging becomes something desired, rather than imposed.

It is no surprise that often children in their teenage years kick against the faith they have been brought up with. This faith needs to become their choice and not the imposition of parents. That challenging age in which they are making choices themselves is so important. It is so important for parents not to hold to the imposition of faith too tightly, but rather to let their children go and grow in their own faith. But that can lead to some difficult times.

My cousin James was a good friend. He was a couple of years younger than me, but we enjoyed time together. I was at home when the phone call came: James had been killed on his little motor bike, along with his girlfriend who was riding pillion. He was just 17. James had one artificial hand and it seemed he lost control and went into the back of a skip parked in the road. The funeral service will stay in my mind forever. The first part was held at the premises of a church both James and his girlfriend attended. The pastor painted a picture of these two as fine young Christians and assured us they were now in glory. The committals were separate and the leader of my aunt's church spoke much more realistically of James, who at the time of the accident was going through many doubts and wobbles in his faith. My aunt wrestled for years with whether or not James was "saved". If the definition the pastor gave was to be the answer, then he was not! But the honesty of my aunt's definition recognised the issue far more clearly: James grew up with faith, but the growing was challenged by his youthful adolescence. The reality of his faith, as for the faith of all of us, is between us and the Lord, who alone knows our hearts.

You see it's not about names on a human list, but names on God's heart. And he has the children on his heart -he loves them. We need to honour that by thanking God for them, not just at birth but time and time again and by valuing them in the way we include them in church, bless them with the best of our time and effort in church, and pray constantly for them to grow in their faith even as we are growing in ours. For me, including them with their family in the communion service is entirely appropriate and something I have loved to encourage. Even if a church decides that communion is only for those of a certain age, or those who have been baptised, or confirmed, it is vital they still make every effort to include the children within the kingdom and do not make them feel that they are excluded. The Bible speaks of the river, the stream of God's grace, flowing out from heaven's throne. We need to lead our children into the river of faith until they learn to swim themselves and become those who lead others.

So what about baptism? This remains perhaps one of the more challenging issues in church relationships, between those who hold to the practice of infant baptism and confirmation and those who hold to the practice of believers' baptism. For me the two principles I have spoken about are my guidelines. The practice is going to vary, and I cannot find any one practice which I will say is the right one (as opposed to all the others which are wrong!). I have been a practitioner of believer's baptism and, more than that, have held to the principle that believers need to be able to know for themselves the implication of surrendering their lives to Christ to follow him for the rest of their days. But as to what age that means, I remain unwilling to be specific.

My own experience was that at the age of eleven I sat in a church service where baptisms had taken place. I heard a call from the front for others to be baptised and felt compelled to respond. I remember telling my mother who wisely did not try to influence my mind, but suggested I talked to the minister for myself. I cycled to his house; I had never been to the "manse" before. I was ushered into this big study, where I told Samuel Nash that I wanted to be baptised. I cannot recall all that followed, except that we had some classes and then on Easter Sunday I was baptised, still aged eleven. I look back to that moment of baptism as something I chose, I decided and I went through, but also as something God called me to, God wanted for me, and so I needed to be faithful to that promise. I have understood far more since that this was all of God's grace, God's love poured out on me, and the experience of my baptism has been a source of encouragement often in my life.

However it happens and whenever it happens, baptism is there to remind us and the world of the grace of God! When I worked as a hospital chaplain, included in our volunteer team was an Anglican man well into his older years. He nearly always introduced himself as "I'm John and I am a Christian, owned by God since the day I was baptised." I thought at the time it was a strange introduction, but I think he was trying to communicate that, though he was there as a fellow human being, sharing in the sufferings of others, he was also there as God's man, God's ambassador, sharing with them the faith and hope we have in Jesus. Baptism marks us out! John writes in his first letter: *"How great is the love the Father has lavished on us, that we should be called children of God. And that is what we are"* (1 John 3:1).

Our curiosity as adults is just an extension of our curiosity as children, and forever we remain as children of God, loving him with all our hearts and seeking Him with all our minds. I love the vision of heaven painted by the Old Testament prophet Zechariah, *"The city streets will be filled with boys and girls playing there"* (Zechariah 8:5). Heaven will be one great big kids club!

I have a strong sense also that our attitude towards children and especially our willingness to "include" them will shape our attitude to others in the adult world who can so easily be seen as outsiders. Jesus went out of his way to include not only children, but the groups of people who were seen by the religious authorities as not good enough to be included: lepers (Luke 4:12-13), tax collectors (Luke 4:27-28), prostitutes (Luke 7:37-50), and even Roman soldiers (Luke 7:1-10). In the story of Jesus and the centurion (a senior officer in the Roman army) Jesus remarks that *"I have not found such great faith even in Israel"* (Luke 7:9). We need to remember that faith is not about head knowledge of certain doctrines, it is trust in Jesus! We may be surprised to find faith in those who can often be thought of as outsiders to church.

The issue of children and faith really does matter as we seek to bring the Good News of Jesus to a generation of children who, for the most part, have very little connection with the Christian faith. This is a matter of practical importance for all of us as we relate to children, but it is also a matter of theology, what we believe about God and children, and how we understand the Bible's teaching. So let's turn to the subject of theology.

Theology

Now there is a word to turn you off, and make you skip the next few pages. But hang on for a moment and let me try to convince you otherwise! Theology simply means "God-words" and is the term used to talk about the content of our faith. If the "word" of God is so important, God speaking to us as part of the conversation we have with him, then exploring the meaning of those words is also important as part of our curiosity about God.

When I was at college studying Theology, I remember having to write an essay early on in the course, on the subject of the atonement. The word "atonement" didn't mean much to me at the time, and it is still one I would avoid using in conversation with people today. Despite its use as a film title, taken from the book of the same name by Ian McEwan, it is a word most people would struggle to understand. In the New

Testament it occurs only once in Paul's letter to the Romans, twice in the book of Hebrews and twice in John's first letter (Romans 3:25: Hebrews 2:17; Hebrews 9:5: 1 John 2:2; 4:10). It relates back to the Old Testament where the Day of Atonement was part of the sacrificial system which signified God's forgiveness of people's sins. This became the start of its meaning in the New Testament: *"This is love: not that we loved God, but that he loved us and sent his Son as an atoning sacrifice for our sins"* (1 John 4:10).

The atonement has everything to do with restoring a broken relationship (which is actually the theme of the book/film).This is the key concept, more important than any religious talk of a past sacrifice. So other translators of the John passage have chosen to use different words in place of "atoning sacrifice": *"This is love: not that we have loved God, but that he loved us and sent his Son to be the payment for our sins"* (1 John 4:10 God's Word Translation.), *"This is what love is: it is not that we have loved God, but that he loved us and sent his Son to be the means by which our sins are forgiven"* (1 John 4:10 Good News Bible.).

This concept is right at the heart of being a Christian. It is about what Jesus has done so we might be "saved", another word about which we might be curious. When the Alpha course was written in 1990, Nicky Gumbel, the author, included a section titled, "*Why did Jesus die?*". In this chapter he covers the same ground that I went over when I wrote my essay at the start of my theology degree. There are what Christian writers have called, "the four theories of the atonement". The "Classical" theory is about Jesus defeating the enemy on the cross and setting us free from the Devil's control. The "Sacrificial" theory goes back to the Old Testament and sees Jesus as the perfect sacrifice for our sins. The "Legal" theory takes us to the law courts and understands that Jesus has paid the penalty imposed on us for our sins (often called the "Substitutionary" theory). The "Moral" theory looks at the heart of God, who loves the world because of Jesus, and through His love, wins our hearts in repentance and faith.

Over the years that I have been seeking to share the Good News of Jesus, I have heard teaching and read books focusing on each of these. Some of them stood out as extremely powerful, in the way they communicated the message. I think of a message from an American preacher, CJ Mahaney, on Isaiah 53, speaking of the "Substitutionary" theory of atonement. I think of a book by Max Lucado, "*He chose the nails – what God did to win your heart?"*,which explores the "Moral" theory.[25] There has been controversy over the idea that God would deliberately cause his son to suffer, and there has been concern about an overtly militant interpretation, which can seem to emphasise the victory of power rather than the power of love. But all this debate has for me enriched my understanding and grown my faith. I know without a doubt that at the heart of our faith is the event we call the cross. It stands unique in human history: no other death has led to such life. All the theories have something to say that matters. If left standing on their own each of them is in danger of leading us into legalism, whereby we think we are right and others are wrong.

I have recently come across a very challenging book by Nadia Bolz-Weber titled, *"Cranky Beautiful Faith"*. The book cover describes this very personal account of faith as *"edgy outrageous and above all real"*. I am sure some readers would be offended by her language, but there is an undeniable authenticity to her faith and how it grew in her spirit. A chapter

[25] Lucado, M. (2012). *He Chose the Nails*. Thomas Nelson; Reprint edition

titled, *"Clinical Pastoral Education"*, relates how she spent time during her training for the Lutheran Pastorate as a hospital chaplain, facing some heart breaking situations of tragedy. She wondered over the normal Christian responses she had heard to such situations, such as, *"God has a plan, we just don't know what it is"* or, *"maybe God took your daughter because he needs another angel in heaven."* Though she could in some sense understand why these things were said, to try to give some comfort to the bereaved, she was dissatisfied by them, as indeed I am. The end of her term there coincided with Easter, and on Good Friday she went and listened to passion music sung by the chapel choir and the story of Easter read from John's gospel. She writes, *"I was stunned that Good Friday, by this familiar but foreign story of Jesus' last hours, and I realised that in Jesus, God had come to dwell with us and share our human story. Even the parts of the story that are the most painful"*, and she went on to write one of the most challenging sentences I have ever read describing the cross: *"Maybe the Good Friday story is about how God would rather die than be in our sin-accounting business anymore".*[26] This struck me as

[26] Bolz-Weber, N. (2013). *Cranky Beautiful Faith: For irregular (and regular) people*. Canterbury Press. Used with permission

such an insight. It combines the love of God with the problem of sin, and recognises that God was willing to die to stop us being condemned. It strikes me as a most excellent commentary on Paul's words: *"Therefore there is now no condemnation for those who are in Christ Jesus"* (Romans 8:1).

I remain eagerly curious to explore how this unique event, the death of Jesus, is today the means by which we as human beings alive now can relate personally to God, our Creator and Heavenly Father. And anyone who is seeking to understand their faith, and share it with others, does well to be curious about this amazing reality that the Bible calls "atonement".

My final weeks as a local minister coincided with Easter celebrations, which in our town included a joint churches event in the market square on Good Friday. It fell to me to lead this year, and I was looking for a way to communicate something of this magnificent gift of atonement. There had been quite a few news items of tragedy around that time, and there are always people in a crowd who are in the storm of a tough situation. I felt God say that the key message was about hope in the face of seemingly impossible circumstances. One of the songs more recently added to the church's Easter repertoire is called *"The Power of the Cross"* written by Keith Getty and Stuart Townend.[27]

It has a powerful crescendo in the tune, which combined with the lyrics makes this song highly charged.

The song begins with the darkness of the day Jesus was crucified, the darkness of his physical pain, and the darkness of his spiritual pain. It describes how in his death, Jesus carried all the evil which is in the world and in our own lives. The music slowly amplifies the heaviness of this story, leading to the crescendo of the chorus, Christ becoming sin for us, taking our blame, and taking away the wrath of God, leaving us amazingly forgiven. In the third stanza the writers imagine daylight running away, and the very ground shaking, as Jesus utters his final cry, *"it is finished,"* And then in the fourth verse the deeper meaning of the cross is explained, that through the suffering of Jesus I am released from the grip of death and am free to live, fully and eternally. This is the power of the Cross. Music and words combine to

[27]Getty, K. and Townend, S. (2005). *The Power of the Cross.* Thankyou Music.

communicate both the weight of this world-changing moment, but also the hope it brings.

I wanted to use the song for the event, but needed to start with some other music which might just attract and gain the attention of the people in the market square. My search led me to the opening of the 5th symphony by Gustav Mahler. It begins with loud discordant chords in a minor key, which when played full blast through outdoor loudspeakers would be impossible to ignore! But what also drew me to this music was the title Mahler gave the symphony: *"Funeral march to joy"*. The final movement of the symphony is a dance! This gave me an opportunity to connect the funeral march of Jesus approaching the cross on Good Friday with the joy that resurrection brought to Jesus and his friends on Easter Sunday. It also allowed me to speak of the funeral marches we all take in our lives because of the tragedies that occur, and the joy that will come to us as we believe. That all led perfectly to our singing the song *"The Power of the Cross"*. It was sung with real commitment and authority by the hundreds of Christians who had met in the market square that Good Friday. Theological curiosity is not about denying the faith, it is about asking God to keep showing us more about the faith we have learned, and realising there will always be *"more light and truth to break forth from his word".28*

But there is another area that should spark our curiosity, which is more likely to be a challenge as we seek to communicate with others, both within the faith community and beyond the faith community. And that is the area of science and faith.

Science and faith

If we are to be curious about our faith, and continue to be curious as children of God, science and faith is one area we have to be willing to look into. As I write this another "scientific breakthrough" has been announced. Astrophysicists have at last detected gravitational waves. I was slightly amused by the way the BBC Newscaster said, *"Our correspondent will explain what these waves are and what this discovery will mean for us."* I am reminded of the words of Richard Feynman, the late Nobel Laureate in Physics, who said, *"I think I can safely say that nobody understands quantum mechanics."* In other words, these theoretical discoveries, although supported by

28 Words from a speech by John Robinson given in 1620 as the Pilgrim Fathers set sail in their ship *"The Mayflower"* for America.

highly sophisticated (and expensive) experimentation are always going to remain beyond our complete understanding, simply because they go beyond the time and space in which we live. Knowing that black holes do exist and that they interact with each other, creating gravitational waves, does absolutely nothing to help us cope with the realities of this planet, and of the needs of the people who live on it. And yet curiosity about this world and this universe in which we live is very important, and, for me, a God-given aspect of humanity. Professor Stephen Hawking in his BBC Reith Lecture in February 2016 advised young scientists is to be curious and to keep a sense of wonder about our complex universe and what makes it exist.

What scientific curiosity does for me is to keep me humble before our Creator, and full of astonishment at what God has made. I have never been overly troubled as so many Christians seem to have been by the debate around Creation. The Bible for me so beautifully describes the creation of the world by God: God is the origin of the universe and God gives order to the universe. The first book of the Bible tells us that God spoke, and the stars and planets were made; he spoke, and life was set upon this planet, the flora and fauna by which we continue to be entranced; he spoke and mankind were created. The book of Job in the Old Testament contains some wonderful expressions of this creative spectacle. God asks Job, *"Where were you when I laid the earth's foundation? Tell me, if you understand. Who marked off its dimensions? Surely you know! Who shut up the sea behind doors when it burst forth from the womb, when I made the clouds its garment and wrapped it in thick darkness, when I fixed limits for it and set its doors and bars in place? Have you ever given orders to the morning, or shown the dawn its place, that it might take the earth by the edges and shake the wicked out of it? Have you journeyed to the springs of the sea or walked in the recesses of the deep? Have you comprehended the vast expanses of the earth? Tell me, if you know all this"* (Job 38:1-18). This is poetic language, making it crystal clear that God is behind the universe and all the systems we experience in the natural world. This is not about how God made the heavens and the earth, this is about God, the Creator and Sustainer of life.

The New Testament gives us a clear indication of what it is God is saying to us through creation. He is telling us that he, the Lord, Father, Son and Spirit, exists outside the time and space of the universe. Jesus prayed, *"Father, I want those you have given me to be with me where I am, and to see my glory, the glory you have given me because you loved me before the creation of the world"* (John 17:24). And God is telling us that our relationship with him is not limited to this space-time world, *"For he chose us in him before the creation of the world to be holy and blameless in his sight"* (Ephesians 1:4). He tells us that Jesus, the Son, is Sovereign over this world, *"The Son is the image of the invisible God, the firstborn over all creation"* (Colossians 1:15), and then he tells us that it is always a matter of faith to discover these truths, *"By faith we understand that the universe was formed at God's command, so that what is seen was not made out of what was visible."* (Hebrews11:3).

These are the truths which by faith we understand: God exists beyond our space-time universe, Jesus is Lord over that universe and our relationship with him begins and ends outside that universe; it is by faith we understand these things. Science is not about faith, it is about explaining the factual mechanisms within the universe: how weather works, how cells multiply, how stars and planets move, how life grows— wonderful, curious, extraordinary science. But science is not going to change the faith we have that God is outside this universe and sovereign over it. That is why you will find many scientists, respected in their profession, who are also God-believers. One of those, John Polkinghorne, wrote in the introduction to his book *"Exploring Reality"*, *"Yet its (i.e. Physics) enthralling account is not sufficient by itself to quench our thirst for understanding, for science describes only one dimension of the many layered reality within which we live, restricting itself to the impersonal and general, and bracketing out the personal and unique".*[29]

The biggest problem that does raise its head within our Christian community is that of the theory of Evolution. Very simply stated, because that is how so many Christians will think of it, the scientific explanation of the development of life down millions of year is in direct contradiction to the Genesis description which speaks of creation in six days. This will remain irresolvable, unless we take the whole of the Biblical teaching on creation together rather than just Genesis chapter 1 on its own. These words from the book of Hebrews are a good starting point: *"By faith we understand that the universe was formed at*

[29] Polkinghorne, J. (2005). *Exploring Reality.* SPCK. Permission requested

God's command, so that what is seen was not made out of what was visible" (Hebrews 11:3). They emphasise the need for faith in God as Creator, and of his sovereignty over the process of bringing the material universe into existence from that which is unseen. Peter writes that, *"With the Lord a day is like a thousand years, and a thousand years are like a day"* (2 Peter 3:8). Our concept of time, of *"a day"*, is different from God's; to God, a day can be as a thousand years, and a thousand years as a day. Paul reminds us that, *"we are God's handiwork created in Christ Jesus"* (Ephesians 2:10). The focus for our faith is that everything comes from God and that each of us, as an individual, is a purposeful part of that creation. It is about our relationship with our maker, who is eternal and yet has stepped into time in Jesus, so that we can know him with us, day by day.

John Polkinghorne underlines that for him as a scientist (a fellow of Queens College Cambridge) and a Christian (Canon theologian of Liverpool Cathedral), the key issue in the Evolution debate is not about time but about the distinctiveness of man. We may share 98.4% of our genes with the chimpanzees but the *"qualitative differences correspond to an irreducible novelty of that emergence (of human beings)".[30]* He speaks of how our lives as human beings are vastly different from that of the apes, although we share physical processes and although the apes show some signs of the abilities that we have. He speaks of the significance of what he calls "God-consciousness", something in us which seeks to recognise our dependence upon God.

Professor Stephen Hawking's comment, quoted earlier, that young scientists should continue to be curious and to keep a sense of wonder about our complex universe and what makes it exist, is intriguing. He would not want to understand that curiosity, that sense of wonder, as God-consciousness, but I do! There is something within us which needs to have a sense of where we come from and where we belong. So far in this section on science and faith I have been writing of the physical sciences, but there is a growing recognition that what matters for us as people is as much to be found in the psychological sciences.

[30] Ibid.

108

When I began in ministry, mental health issues were put into rigid boxes of definition, and the people who suffered from them put in human boxes of psychiatric institutions. Thankfully, very thankfully, we have as a society moved away from both fixed definitions of mental illness and such rigid treatments. But the result is we are all more aware of difficulties in mental health. All of us will know someone who suffers to some degree from a depressive illness or from personality issues. I hesitate to use more words as the descriptions of these conditions vary so much. As believers too we are slowly becoming aware of the need for much better mental health care, and the place of prayer for healing, not just of physical illness but of mental, emotional illness too.

All this very deliberately points to the unique nature of humanity within the created world. It is this reality we need to defend and explain. Many centuries ago the Christian theologian Augustine (354-430AD) wrote words which have been quoted ever since, *"Thou hast made us for Thyself, O Lord, and our heart is restless until it finds its rest in Thee."*[31] Rather less well known are these words attributed to Augustine:*"To*

[31] Augustine of Hippo, *Confessions*

fall in love with God is the greatest romance; to seek Him the greatest adventure; to find Him, the greatest human achievement."[32] The need which so many people have for a sense of meaning and of understanding of themselves, let alone of their place in society, is met in a relationship with the God who made us and who in Jesus shared our humanity, so that we might find ourselves as "children of God."

I remain utterly curious about the world God has made. I read about the latest scientific theories with fascination and amazement (more than with comprehension!); nothing I read shakes my faith in God's existence or in God's significance for me. It only makes me pray more that people's eyes would be *"enlightened"*, as Paul prays, so that they might *"know him better"* (Ephesians 1:18).

My curiosity in science leads me to want to talk with others about the wonder of God as Creator. But there is another subject which is far more likely to be on their minds, and that is the subject of suffering. If God made us, and loves us, why do we suffer so? Now there's a question!

[32] Attributed to Augustine of Hippo, source unknown

Suffering

When something tragic, disastrous and unexpected happens the question that is always asked is "Why?". It is a question that comes from deep within our being; it not simply a question about what caused the event, but what is the reason behind the event. I have lived through many such events, some very personal and some shared with the wider national and international community. Personally, I first encountered the issue when my mother died after a basic surgical procedure, when I was 17 years old. She had an undiagnosed infection which led to her being in a near comatose state after the surgery, a state in which she remained for three months before dying of pneumonia. I visited her often on the way to school or on the way home as the hospital was on my cycle route. I told her about my new girlfriend, Monica (who I eventually married), but I don't know if she heard or understood. The church we were part of prayed, and prayed more, holding special prayer meetings at the church premises. One day a church leader came and prayed at her bedside, anointing her with oil, as the Bible says in James 5:14, but she died. I remember a little of the thanksgiving service: not so much about what was said, but what was sung. We sung *"Thine be the glory risen conquering Son, endless is the victory Thou o'er death hast won."* I cannot sing that hymn without choking; it always touches the deepest chords in my soul, because in it was and is the merging of awful pain and of strong faith. I have often wished my mum could have been alive when I was married, when our children were born, when I was very ill, when life was hard, and when grief was very real. But though that longing for her to be alive was and still is genuine, so was and is faith; faith that there is a victory over death in Jesus in whom I believe.

Exactly the same issues arise in the wider suffering with which we are faced in the wars, the earthquakes, the terrorist attacks, the sickness and accidents about which we hear all the time. Sometimes they are utterly dominant, as for example when planes were flown into the buildings in America in 9-11 2001, or more recently in the attacks on Paris and Brussels, Nice and Berlin, and throughout Turkey. By now as you read this there will have been another such event. Earthquakes make the news for a week or so and then are all too easily forgotten. Then there are the wars, the utterly futile loss of life, caused in the most horrific manner by airstrikes and suicide bombers. And even more heartbreakingly, simply because of the unexpected nature of the suffering, there are those tragic accidental events, often in ships, planes or cars. In every one of these cases there is a matter of fact answer to the question "why?": the earth's plates moved, there was a fault in the machine, someone decided to fire a weapon or release a bomb or to cause mayhem. But the question of "why?" goes deeper than these facts. The question is about why this life which we expected to go on, and be happy and fulfilling, has been devastated or ended by this event.

I have read many books on this theme, all of which seek to explore this question. The writers are curious, as I am. It is all too easy to ask the question "why?" but not think further about what it really means. The problem with the question is that it is based on the premise that we have the "right" to a long and happy life. If this does not happen, then someone must be blamed and so we ask "Why?" But what is this "right"? And if we have a right to a long and happy life, who gave it to us? If nobody gave it to us, then maybe we don't have that right at all? But if someone gave it to us, that someone has to be God. So we blame God, which is about as far as many people get.

Sydney Carter wrote songs that sought to explore the questions of life. One of his most enduring songs is "*Lord of the Dance*", which speaks of Jesus' death and resurrection in the words, *"They cut me down but I leapt up high, I am the life that will never, never die"*.[33] But another of his songs, *"Friday Morning"*, explores further the death of Jesus. It is written from the point of view of one of the criminals who was sentenced to be crucified along with Jesus. It says, *"It was on a Friday morning that they took me from the cell, and I saw they had a carpenter to crucify as well. You can blame it on Pilate, You can blame it on the Jews, You can blame it on the Devil, but it's God that I accuse. It's God they ought to crucify instead of you and me I said to the carpenter, a-hanging on the tree"*.[34] That's not a song I would choose to sing today. It could be said to be anti-Semitic, and that's a road down which none of us want to travel. But, more than that, it only gets as far as the conclusion that, if God is behind it all, then it's God who is to blame. We need to go further than that. The Carter song hints that there was something very strange actually going on there: that it was God who was in Jesus being crucified. But our faith declares this to be the truth, it was in fact God they were crucifying! Our faith is absolutely that in Jesus

[33] Carter, S. (1963). *Lord of the Dance.* London: Stainer and Bell. Used with permission
[34] Carter, S. (1959). *Friday Morning.* Stainer and Bell. Used with permission.

God has given his life for us, to restore to us to himself. He has, through the death and resurrection of Jesus, given us, not the right to a long and happy life on earth, but *"the right to become children of God"* (John 1:12).

John goes on in his letter to say, *"See what great love the Father has lavished on us, that we should be called children of God! And that is what we are! The reason the world does not know us is that it did not know him. Dear friends, now we are children of God, and what we will be has not yet been made known. But we know that when Christ appears, we shall be like him, for we shall see him as he is"* (1 John 3:1-2). There are two crucial concepts in these words. The first is the underlying truth of God's love. If we love someone we will share in their pain. We will cry with them, sit with them, hold them, and above all simply be with them. And God, who deeply loves us, is with us in our pain. Jesus totally demonstrates that as he suffered so much. All these aspects of curiosity come back to a fundamental revelation given to us throughout the Bible, in the whole of the Gospel of Jesus, and by the Spirit down the ages: that God is love. Love is the one dimension in humanity which defies scientific explanation—however much the scientists can find out how our brain chemistry works. Love is a choice, it is a reality, it is obvious by its fruits, it is vulnerable, it is fragile, and yet it is incredibly strong and resilient. And love comes from God, lavished on us, in Jesus, to the extent that he bears our pain. We are coming back to the curiosity I spoke of in Theology and especially in the atonement. It is far more than a few words can express or explore, but the more we realise God loves us enough to die for us, the more we are going to be able to deal with the suffering of this world.

The second concept conveyed in these words is that by our faith we become children of God, and our life now and in the future is totally bound up in being with Jesus. Life is not to be valued by its length or its happiness here and now, it is to be valued by our existence as children of God, now and always, which is why, for me, the response to this question of "why suffering?" is always the presence of Jesus. I want to bring people who are suffering into the presence of Jesus, and when I am suffering I want my brothers and sisters to bring me into the presence of Jesus. One of the greatest privileges of ministry is to be able to comfort people in their suffering. And we do so not by our words but by his presence. You see, if we bring people to Jesus, and they know, by faith, that he is with them, then it follows that he is alive, and the truth of the hymn words *"endless is the victory thou o'er death hast won"* are vindicated.[35]

These two concepts are to be found in the most powerful book on the subject of suffering, a book which is more than a book, as it is part of the Bible: the book of Job. What is remarkable is that here, centuries before Jesus came, there is a questioning sufferer, Job, who has a faith strong enough to say, *"I know that my redeemer lives, and that in the end he will stand on the earth. And after my skin has been destroyed, yet in my flesh I will see God; I myself will see him with my own eyes—I, and not another. How my heart yearns within me!"* (Job 19:25-27). Job still is curious about his suffering, curious enough to challenge the views of his so-called friends, who put all his sufferings down to his own sinfulness. Job refutes this strongly, and rightly. We have been told at the start of the book that Job was *"blameless and upright; he feared God and shunned evil"* (Job 1:1). It is never all right for us to blame someone for their own suffering. Of course there are consequences which follow from our actions—our life style choices, our

[35] Budry, E. Trans: Hoyle, B R. (1904). *Thine Be the Glory.*

behaviour and our words—and sometimes those consequences are painful. But that argument on its own will not suffice to explain the suffering in this world. There is so much that clearly is not related one bit to the previous actions of the victim.

The question "why?" is not answered either by the basic forensic explanation of the event, or by saying that it was deserved because of some failure in the victim. Jesus confirms this when he was asked whether the eighteen people killed when a tower in Jerusalem collapsed (a news story of that day) were more guilty than all the other residents of Jerusalem who were not killed. He said, *"I tell you, no!"* (Luke 13:5). Again, this doesn't mean that we are all innocent before God, indeed Jesus goes on to underline that we all need to turn back to God. But it does mean that we can never make a simple equation which assumes we deserve all that we suffer. Job's friends tried to do this and God's comment to them was *"I am angry with you and your two friends because you have not spoken the truth about me as my servant Job has"* (Job 42:7). Job does not know why he is suffering, but he has faith that God is sovereign, and that, whatever the reason for the suffering, God has his hand on Job for good.

It takes some faith to believe that when you're going through the sort of thing Job went through: the loss of his livelihood through enemy attack, the death of his children through a violent storm, and the loss of his dignity through an attack of painful sores, *"from the soles of his feet to the crown of his head"* (Job 2:7). Job was unaware of the debate between God and Satan, which lay behind the suffering (see Job chapter 1). All Job could do was trust, and that is what he did do. In the end he even repents before God for trying to work it all out, and he repeats again what his faith has held to throughout, *"I know that you can do all things; no purpose of yours can be thwarted"* (Job 42:2). We know as we read the start of the book of Job that the real issue at stake here is whether or not Job will continue to have faith if he suffers, or whether he will curse God (Job 1:11). That is still the issue we all face as we consider suffering: will we trust God or will we curse God?

But there is a deeper reality to the story of Job, and that is Job's relationship with God. His faith is not just in an absent Sovereign but in a present God. Even when he cries out through his suffering and asks "where are you God?" he is doing so out of his relationship with God. Though he cannot feel God's presence he affirms it in his desire for God to answer him. And of course God does: *"Then the Lord spoke to Job out of the storm"* (Job 38:1).

So whether the suffering is intensely personal, as it may be for you now, or extremely public, as no doubt it will continue to be in the affairs of our messed up world, the only way to begin to approach it is to seek to bring God alongside—the Father who loves us, the Son who took our pain, and the Spirit who is our comforter.

Curiosity leads us to ask the question, but faith leads us to trust Jesus is with us. My conviction is that as we continue to explore the question, and apply our faith, that faith will grow. The writer Timothy Keller has written a most helpful book on this theme titled, *"Walking with God through Pain and Suffering".*[36] The title is key: if we are to cope with the deepest cries of hurt in our lives and the lives of others around us, we have to walk with God. The conversation we have with the Lord in our daily lives is going to be the vital faith-building for the days when we cannot pray a word but need God so much. Another writer, Ronald

[36] Keller, T. (2013). *Walking with God through Pain and Suffering.* Hodder and Stoughton

Dunn, is perhaps best known for a book on prayer called *"Don't just stand there, pray something"*. But for me his most helpful book is *"When heaven is silent"*. The book starts with the personal story of the death of one of his children by suicide. [37] What he writes is steeped in a deep personal faith through which he has habitually conversed with God. This is turn has grown his faith so he is able to keep trusting God even when heaven seems to be silent. As Christians we do not have pat answers to the problem of suffering. No book can offer a solution that fits every situation. What we do have is faith in God who longs to be with us. I remain endlessly curious about how God works in our lives for good, especially when life is tough. I have my own list of heroes of faith (a little like the list God has given us in Hebrews chapter 11). These are people I have known personally who suffered through illness, tragedy, false accusations, and yet displayed a faith that grew through the difficulties. The truth is that, the more curious we are to know God throughout our lives, the more our faith grows.

[37] Dunn, R. (1994). *When Heaven is Silent: How God Ministers to Us Through the Challenges of Life.* Paternoster Press/Authentic Publishing; New edition

The issue of suffering leads us to the last area where I want us to be curious! So here is another question to consider:

Are we there yet?

That's a question all of us asked when we were children, on a journey to visit our grandparents, or on a trip to the seaside. We knew there was a destination, but we had very little perspective as to how far the journey was, or how long it would take, so we continued to ask, "Are we there yet?" The same is true in our lives as followers of Jesus, as we keep our faith growing, but we do not have a clear idea of how long it will take!

Right at the end of the account of Jesus' life on earth, after the resurrection, before Jesus ascended to be with the Father, John tells us how Jesus met his friends by the Sea of Galilee. First he fed them physically, preparing bread on a beach fire, and showing the frustrated fishermen where to put their nets to find a huge shoal of fish. Then he fed them with grace, especially Peter, who had denied his association with Jesus on the night of Jesus' trial. There was no rebuke of Peter, just a welcome and a call to keep following. Jesus said to Peter, *"when you* are old you will stretch out your hands, and someone else will dress you and lead you where you do not want to go" (John 21:18). John then comments on these words as he writes, "Jesus said this to indicate the kind of death by which Peter would glorify God. Then he said to him, 'Follow me'" (John 21:19). So Peter knew that he would get old (I wonder, what age that meant!) But then Peter noticed John standing there. John was probably Peter's best friend, and Peter wanted to know what was going to happen to him so he asked Jesus, "Lord, what about him?" (John 21:21). Jesus' reply is so helpful to us: "If I want him to remain alive until I return what is that to you? You must follow me" (John 21:22). For each of us the question, "are we there yet?" has a completely different personal answer. And yet it is not one which we are going to be able to know. God knows, and that is all we need to know!

There are two consequences of this which must be part of our growing faith. The first is that God is still working in our lives, every day we have breath. We are not yet complete, so must keep growing! And the second is that God alone knows how long our life will be, and how long it will be before Jesus returns. Our response is not to keep asking "are we there yet?" but rather keep saying "yes" to his call, *"follow me."*

The last day of term at school remains for me a clear memory: the last school assembly, a game of pirates in the gym when all the gym equipment was out, a good old fashioned game of chase, and the same old ditty: "No more days of sin, no more days of sorrow, no more days in this old dump we're breaking up tomorrow!" Somehow the fact that we would be back in a few weeks' time didn't feature in our thinking! But the day eventually came when we not only broke up from school, but we finished with school forever. However, when it comes to the school of grace, to our lives as followers of Jesus, none of us has finished yet!

Fifteen years ago one of the books which opened my eyes to some of the "more" of God, was *"Messy Spirituality"* by Mike Yaconelli. My copy is very well worn, and contains a piece of paper with my notes of sections in the book which affected me deeply when I first read it. Mike wrote, *"When we seek God, Jesus begins to take shape in our lives. He begins a good work in us, but the finishing process is a more-than-a-lifetime process... Jesus understood unfinishedness very well,* which is why he was comfortable leaving eleven unfinished disciples".[38] He recounted a "Peanuts" cartoon where Charlie Brown stopped for advice at Lucy's 5 cent psychology booth. She told him, *"Life is like a deck chair Charlie, on the cruise ship of life, some people place their deck chair at the rear of the ship so they can see where they've been. Others place their deck chair at the front of the ship so they can see where they're going."*[39] Then Lucy asked Charlie Brown which way his deck chair was facing. His reply was, *"Heck, I can't get my deck chair unfolded"* (For those unfamiliar with the deck chair, it is a chair made of a wooden frame with a striped canvas material seat, which folds flat. The process of putting this chair into its upright position is notoriously puzzling!). Mike's point was that for most of us our "spirituality" is not yet put together. We certainly have not finished our "faith-growing".

There are many books written by Christian writers (and this could be said to be one of them), which tend to make us feel we are not where we should be, or what we should be, as a Christian. Perhaps "should

[38] Yakonelli, M. (2001). *Messy Spirituality: Christianity for the rest of us.* Hodder and Stoughton. Permission requested
[39] Charles M. Schulz, *The Complete Peanuts*, Vol. 16: 1981-1982

be" is the wrong phrase. If we said, "we are not yet where we will be, or what we will be", then we are being far more true to the testimony of the Bible. John again, this time writing when he was older to the Christians who were facing all sorts of challenges to their faith, said, *"Dear friends, now we are children of God, and what we will be has not yet been made known"* (1 John 3:2). Faith needs to keep growing.

Paul writes about this in his letter to the Ephesians. He speaks of the function of the combined ministries of apostles, prophets, evangelists, pastors and teachers as *"equipping God's people for works of service, so that the body of Christ may be built up until we all reach unity in the faith and in the knowledge of the Son of God and become mature, attaining to the whole measure of the fullness of Christ"* (Ephesians 4:12-13). The question is; have we yet reached this maturity?

Paul was speaking to the church as a whole, and it would be obvious to any of us looking at "church" in its widest meaning of "all the believers" that we are not yet fully mature. We have not yet reached unity in the faith. If we think of "church" as one local gathering of believers, again no "church" would claim it has arrived. We are seeking all the time to add to "church" new believers who themselves are not yet mature, even if we think we might be. So what about ourselves? Have we arrived? Mike Yakonelli quotes the words of Henri Nouwen, *"He who thinks that he is finished is finished. Those who think that they have arrived have lost their way"*.[40]

If this is true then the challenge to us all is to keep growing in our faith, to keep finding out more, being filled more with the Holy Spirit, becoming more like Jesus. Either we are to do that or we are to give up. I find the greatest sadness in those who have been actively part of the organisation of church and yet have not been growing in their faith, not been drawn to be curious, to ask and seek, to explore what the Bible is saying, what God may be speaking into their lives. Some like that are among those who have drifted away. When "church" no longer appeals to them, or gives them the sense of significance that comes from having a job etc., they cease to be part of it.

Since I have retired from my role as a church leader, I have found great delight in continuing to explore

[40] Nouwen, H J M. (1981). *The Genesee Diary*. Darton, Longman & Todd. Used with permission

aspects of faith and following Jesus. This book itself is part of that process. I remind you of what John Robinson said in his address to the pilgrims who were about to set sail for a new life in America on the ship Mayflower: *"I am verily persuaded the Lord hath more truth and light yet to break forth from His Holy Word".* Can it be true that God has yet more light and truth to break forth from his Word? Wasn't his Word fixed, as it were, clear for all to see? Isn't the idea of "new truth" rather dangerous? Isn't that the source of heresy down the ages? Yet over the years as I have had the great privilege of seeking to teach others, I have found that there is indeed always more light and truth breaking out of God's word because, as we have already discovered, God is in the business of conversation, and conversation is not simply repeating yesterday's words, but speaking fresh today.

In my lifetime there have been significant moments when fresh "word" from God has broken out. Revival movements have sprung up, each offering us fresh insights into the working of God in our lives, the power of his Spirit to transform our lives and the grace of his love to shape our lives. God has spoken through men and women from different nations, challenging our faith. My own list includes Dietrich Bonhoeffer, a German Pastor killed by the Nazis just before the end of the war, whose book *"Letters and Papers from Prison"* inspired me beyond words to be a follower of Jesus.[41] It includes Josef Ton, a pastor from Romania who I first met at college in 1969, and challenged me with the priority of loving Jesus first before all. On the list is Mike Huck, a pastor from the North of England, pioneering new ways of being church long before the arrival of "Fresh Expressions" or "Emerging Church". I think of the refreshing way Terry Virgo expounded the stories of the Old Testament, and the way Heidi Baker spoke of the Healing Power of God, especially among the poor in Mozambique where she and her husband worked. I have always had this curious nature, and I believe it is something essential for any growing Christian. I am so thankful for so many people in my life who have stirred me, challenged me, upset me and sometimes even annoyed me. Because in the process I have found a desire to keep finding out more of God's heart.

So we have not arrived yet, but when will we arrive? Jesus' words to Peter when he wanted to know the

---

[41] Bonhoeffer, D. (1951). *Letters and Papers from Prison.*

future for his friend John made it clear that the future is in God's hands. In the same context, the time between Jesus' resurrection and his ascension to the Father, Luke records how the disciples asked Jesus, *"Lord, are you at this time going to restore the kingdom to Israel?"* (Acts 1:6). This conveyed the political aspiration of the people of Israel to be free from Roman rule and once again be a nation state. Jesus' answer is so important for us: *"It is not for you to know the times or dates the Father has set by his own authority"* (Acts 1:7).

So why is it that Christians continue to speculate about the time when Jesus will return? So much effort has been expended on what people call "the end times." Much of it focuses around the book of Revelation in the Bible. I have been curious about this book, and have read many of the commentaries which have been written down the years. It seems to me that the message of Revelation, painted in dramatic pictures, is quite simply, "The game is not over yet! But when the final whistle blows, Jesus' team will be victorious!"

At the time the book was written, the Christians were being persecuted and some of them were being killed. There were forces opposed to the Gospel which seemed to be throttling the young church, squeezing the life out of it. But John writes to tell them that in heaven there is a "*Lion*": "*Do not weep! See the Lion of the tribe of Judah, the Root of David, has triumphed*" (Revelation 5:5). There follows a series of dramas each with the same message, that God knows what is going on, he has authority over what is going on, and in the end his kingdom will prevail. But although the message of ultimate triumph is very strong, so too is the constant reminder that the way the Lion has conquered is as a Lamb! The paradox of our Christian faith is that Jesus won by losing. He triumphed over death by dying. The power of his victory is in his blood, his life, given for us. And so we, whatever the threat against us, can know that God is in charge, and that we will overcome, "*by the blood of the lamb*" (Revelation 12:11). Our response to the uncertainty of life, to the seemingly growing power of evil in the world, is not to be one of human power or military might, but to be that of love, the love of God, working in and through us. There is a call in the book of Revelation to "*patient endurance and faithfulness on the part of God's people*" (Revelation 13v10) and to confidence in the promise of Jesus, "*Yes, I am coming soon*" (Revelation 22:20).

So what do we say to the child in the back seat of the car who keeps asking us, "Are we there yet?" We say, "no, but we will be soon!" Soon simply means we're not there yet, but we're on the way! And that is how Jesus answers our question, "Are we there yet?" When it comes to the "end times", our response must always be to seek to keep growing in faith, and to leave off the speculation about times and dates. I wonder (part of my curious nature) why people so want to know the future? Surely the better way to live is to be content in the present. I listened recently to an athlete who was taking part in the Paralympics in Brazil. An accident had deprived this person of the freedom to walk, but they were determined to keep active and continue to strive to achieve their dreams. So they had taken up wheelchair racing and wheelchair skiing, and indeed achieved very high results. Their message to others was to keep going for their dreams. For the vast majority of people, dreams are not about the Olympics, or climbing high mountains, or creating a successful business. These things might be possible for some but are always going to be reserved for just a very few. Most people need dreams that are about today, about finding contentment in the things we can do, we can say, or we can be, this day. As Christians we do have an ultimate dream! My friend Stan said his prayer was "make me more like Jesus", and John's letter provides the promise that, *"When Christ appears we shall be like him for we shall see him as he is"* (1 John 3:2). If that is our ultimate dream, then my contentment each day is to somehow live in a way that reflects Jesus to those around me.

This chapter began with the importance of asking questions. Whether we are asking about the faith of our children, the mystery of the Cross, the relationship between science and faith, the reason for suffering, or when will it all end, the underlying truth is that we believe in God who holds all of this in his hands. And as we ask and express our curiosity, this God longs to speak with us, not always giving us the exact answers we want, but always assuring us of his presence with us and of his ultimate control over these issues.

Jesus said, *"The wind blows wherever it pleases. You hear its sound, but you cannot tell where it comes from or where it is going. So it is with everyone born of the Spirit"* (John 3:8). There is always something "beyond us" in the ways of God and the work of the Spirit. Paul in Romans expresses this very well when he says, *"Oh, the depth of the riches of the wisdom and knowledge of God! How unsearchable his judgments, and his paths beyond tracing out!"* (Romans 11:33). There always needs to be room for wonder at the ways of God, and that means humility to recognise that we have more to receive and more to understand. To ask for more of the Spirit is not to ask for more excitement or more power for us, but for more faith in the wisdom and knowledge of God, a greater sense of awe in his presence and a greater trust that he is at work. As Paul went on to say, *"For from him and through him and for him are all things. To him be the glory for ever! Amen"* (Romans 11:36).

Chapter 3

Connections

I have a vivid memory of a trip to Romania in the 1980's when it was still a communist country ruled by the Dictator Nicolai Ceausescu. There were three of us travelling, Richard, Jim and myself. The only airline available at that time was the Romanian State company Tarom, notoriously unreliable! The flight involved a short trip from Heathrow to Brussels, and then a change of plane for the trip to Bucharest. At Brussels we had to leave the plane and wait in the airport lounge for the connecting flight. Richard and I dutifully did as we were told, but Jim, who was not a seasoned traveller, wandered off! When the bus came to pick us up and take us out onto the apron to board the aircraft Jim was nowhere to be seen. We decided to carry on and hope he found his way on time! On board we could see out of the window that the stairs to our plane were still in position, the crew seemed to be waiting for something. And then an airport service vehicle appeared and out stepped Jim, to board the aircraft. There were mutterings from some about the delay (though to be honest we were already a couple of hours behind schedule!), as we gave looks to say, "He's not with us!" Making the right connections is very important!

A few days later, whilst in Bucharest, Jim set off on his own to find an apartment somewhere in the city suburbs. He had been writing to a resident of the apartment for some years. It was a Bible study correspondence course that had been established for Christians in countries like Romania so they could be encouraged by fellow believers abroad. Jim had been faithfully receiving letters from this person and sending back replies. We have no idea how Jim found his way to the flat, but he did, and he met his pen friend. When he returned to us he had a fresh spring in his step and a light in his eyes. What had been a connection through correspondence was now a connection in person and it meant the world to Jim (and probably to his friend in Bucharest as well). Connections are important and personal connections even more so.

A former principal of the Bible College where I studied, Paul Fiddes, has written a book called, *"Participating in God: a pastoral doctrine of the Trinity."* Writing about his book in an article for the Baptist Missionary Society magazine, he says, *"The*

Trinity is an immensely practical doctrine. It awakens us to notice that we live in a universe which is full of relationships. Everything is connected to everything else, and everyone is connected to everyone else, as the human and physical sciences keep on telling us".[42] His contention is that God is always living *"in eternal relations of love",* the Father loving the Son and the Son loving the Father and the Spirit coming from the Father to bring that love to the Son and to invite the world to share in that love. It is a theme about which we would do well to be curious! Fiddes says, *"The Trinity is not celestial mathematics, but love at the heart of the universe".*[43] It defies our mathematical formulae. It is not a case of 3 in 1, but it is a case of "One" living in eternal relationship with the other "Ones", a relationship into which we ourselves are invited to share.

Or to put it differently, God is full of connections and he longs for us to connect with him, with each other and with the world that he loves so much. So if our faith is to grow, then this will be part of that growth, a growing awareness that we are connected to God, and

[42] Baptist Missionary Society Catalyst magazine Issue 4 2016

[43] Fiddes, P. (2000). *Participating in God: A Pastoral Doctrine of the Trinity.* Article in BMS Catalyst Magazine. Used with permission

that because of that connection we are to connect together with others who are connected to God, and that we are to seek to connect to those who as yet are not connected to him!

Our conversation with God is all about our relationship with him, our connecting to him. Our connecting to others who share our faith is what we call church, and our connecting to those who do not yet share that faith is what we call evangelism. How much simpler would it be if we saw all this together as a natural part of our growing faith?

Church is not an organisation we join, it is the connections we have and cultivate because we are connected to God. And evangelism is not something we do, it is the connections we have and cultivate because we love the Lord, and his love flows from us to those around us.

This book has at its heart the conviction that growing faith matters more than growing church. Over the years I have been aware of just how easy it is to make church the focus of our Christian lives, rather than faith itself. However I want to make it clear that I am not suggesting church does not matter. I am saying simply that if our focus is faith rather than church, then church will grow; but if our focus is church rather than faith we are in danger of falling into all sorts of difficulties. Wherever you are in your faith— just seeking, beginning on the journey of following Jesus, or years down the road of being a Christian, my longing is that you focus on your faith, and growing that faith, rather than worry about whether the church has got it right, whether the church you are part of is doing enough for you, or whether you are doing enough for the church. If you focus on faith growing, rather than church growing, you will keep growing in your faith and you will encourage others to grow in their faith too. Let me repeat Paul's words to the Christians in Corinth: *"Our hope is that, as your faith continues to grow, our sphere of activity among you will greatly expand"* (2 Corinthians 10:15).

Connecting with God is obviously a key part of this growing in faith, hence the first focus of the book is on our conversation with God, but connecting with each other and others is also a part of this growing in faith. Read these two statements from Paul from his letter to the Christians in Ephesus: *"In him the whole building is joined together and rises to become a holy temple in the Lord. And in him you too are being built together to become a dwelling in which God lives by his Spirit"* (Ephesians 2:21-22).

"Instead, speaking the truth in love, we will grow to become in every respect the mature body of him who is the head, that is, Christ. From him the whole body, joined and held together by every supporting ligament, grows and builds itself up in love, as each part does its work" (Ephesians 4:15-16).

Both a building and a body are pictures of the church, the coming together of all the followers of Jesus. Paul writes about *"the whole building"* and *"the whole body"*. This is not about small groups of believers, but all of us, all over the world and from all generations, including those who have lived and died in the faith. There is one building and one body! What a shame we have for so long associated the physical buildings we call church with this one building Paul calls the church. They are just not the same thing! The one building, which is the church of Jesus, is being built – it's not finished yet – of all the bricks, representing you and me and all the other believers. The one body, called the "Body of Christ", is made up of many cells, continually growing and dividing and multiplying.

There is another picture of the church which Paul uses in his Corinthians correspondence, relating to our theme of "growth". He is describing his own work and comparing it to that of a farmer, and he says to his friends in Corinth, *"you are God's field"* (1 Corinthians 3:9). Paul is a farmer, planting the seed of the Good News about Jesus. Other servants of Jesus, like Apollos, have watered the seed, but God has made it grow into a field of wheat. This is the church, a growing, living, thriving community of people, sharing their faith in Jesus as Saviour and Lord, and seeking to be a blessing to the world around them.

We have in our country an organisation called "The Churches Conservation Trust". It describes itself as *"The national charity saving historic churches at risk"*.[44] It is all about preserving old buildings, some of which were built well over 1000 years ago. Many small communities around the country are fighting to save their old church (meaning of course the building) from the ravages of weather, dry rot, woodworm and lack of interest among the villagers. However, if all these buildings were to fall into ruin and end up as piles of rubble, the church would still be alive and

[44] www.visitchurches.org.uk

growing! The building may close, but the coming together of the followers of Jesus is still going to happen.

An idea in the above verses from Ephesians links the two pictures of building and body, and links all of us together! It is contained in a word which is only ever used by Paul in these two verses and literally means "to fit properly together". The building is *"joined together"* and the body is *"joined and held together".* We are not to connect together in some haphazard accidental way, but deliberately, intentionally, finding our place alongside the others who share our faith. And as we do we will grow in our faith, and so will they.

There is a dangerous position into which some are being led, where we give up on church because it is too much of an organisation, and we choose to try to be a follower of Jesus in isolation from others. I have increasingly become aware of people who have their own faith in God, faith in Jesus, faith in the work of the Holy Spirit in their lives, and yet who have abandoned their coming together with other believers. This of course is the very situation the writer to the Hebrews was aware of when writing: *"Let us hold unswervingly to the hope we profess, for he who promised is faithful.*

And let us consider how we may spur one another on toward love and good deeds, not giving up meeting together, as some are in the habit of doing, but encouraging one another—and all the more as you see the Day approaching" (Hebrews 10:23-25). We should notice here how the writer first encourages the Christians to hold to their hope, to be strong in their personal faith and commitment, and then calls them to connect with others, both in practical care and in meeting for mutual encouragement.

I believe that those who have faith but have abandoned the gathering together of believers are in danger. Their faith is not going to grow but may well diminish. The purpose of church is to connect us together to God to help us in our growth in faith. The repeated use of the phrase "one another" in the New Testament should guard us against this isolationism: Jesus' own words to us, *"love one another"* (John 13:34), along with Paul's urging for us to *"be devoted to one another in love: honour one another above yourselves"* (Romans 12:10) should leave us in no doubt that we are to connect to one another in what the Bible calls church. As long as we keep in mind that the goal is to grow in faith, and not to grow the church, then we will find the way to make the progress in our faith that God desires for us.

So let's explore this connecting together. First I want to look at the balance we need between our own personal faith and our faith shared with others. Then I want to look at how we might "do" church in a way that enables the growth God wants. I will consider this under the headings of "The place of the Sunday meeting", "Worship" and "Participation." Finally we will explore how our connections need to include those who as yet do not share our faith, under the heading of "Evangelism."

The balance of individual and shared faith

I have always had a distant longing for Norway. Maybe somewhere in our ancestry "Campion" was a Scandinavian family, rather than a French one as I have tended to assume! A few years ago my wife and I were able to visit the coastal regions of Norway from Bergen to the North Cape, the furthest point north in Europe. What an amazing landscape and, in June, how stunningly beautiful! The Lofoten Islands, way above the Arctic Circle, display meadows of gigantic wildflowers, far taller than usual, produced by the 24 hour daylight of this land of the midnight sun. There is, however, a down-side to the location of this country: very long and dark, winter days with many hours of dismal and dark skies. The bonus of the Northern Lights might sound attractive to us southerners, but the people who live there have had to find ways to manage this challenging climate. Their solution is to balance solitude with community. They seem both to like and need time on their own, content with their own company, and yet they recognise the need for community, and make special effort to engage in social interaction, in celebrations of special occasions.

We tend to think of people as either introverts or extroverts. Of course this is only a generalisation—most of us are somewhere in between the two poles. But considering the whole of humanity, it seems obvious to suggest that we need contentment both in our own company, and in interaction with others. Introverts need to be helped to be able to relate better to others in social activity, and extroverts need to be helped to discover the value of time and space alone.

If we take this into our exploration of Christian faith, it strikes me that there is something very important to discover about the balance of individual faith and shared faith. Jesus knew this—we read of his moments of time-out, so he can be alone with his Father: *"After he had dismissed them, he went up on a mountainside by himself to pray. Later that night, he was there alone"* (Matthew 14:23). And yet we also read of him socialising with his disciples as they walked together, shared meals and relaxed in each other's company: *"One Sabbath Jesus was going through the cornfields, and as his disciples walked along, they began to pick some ears of corn"* (Mark 2:23). But the time spent with his friends was more than just socialising. As he faced his impending arrest by the authorities with the prospect of horrendous suffering, he wanted his friends with him. He poured his heart out to his Father in prayer in the garden of Gethsemane, and then came back to his friends. When he found them sleeping he was really heartbroken by their lack of support: *"Then he returned to his disciples and found them sleeping. 'Couldn't you men keep watch with me for one hour?' he asked Peter"* (Matthew 26:40). The company of believers is vital to us, as is our personal connecting with the Father. It is never "either or", it is always "both".

Bear Grylls, writing of his ascent of Mount Everest said, *"I survived and reached the top of that mountain because of the bonds I had with those beside me, of that*

I am in no doubt. Down that dark crevasse I learned that sometimes we really need each other. We are not designed to be islands. We are made to be connected",

"It was only because our friendships were honest that, time after time, when we were tired or cold or scared we were able to pick ourselves up and keep moving. You don't have to be strong all the time... when we show chinks it creates bonds, and where there are bonds there is strength".[45]

Over the past four decades church attendance in the UK has declined significantly, and many churches in towns and villages of our country have closed. But that trend is being reversed in two quite different ways. The first is in the larger gatherings of people where performance is excellent and the congregation are very much the audience. That is the case both in our city Cathedrals with their high quality classical music sung by choirs and accompanied by organs; and the growing multicultural Mega churches with their contemporary music led by modern worship bands and visual technology. The second way in which the trend is reversed is in the rise of much smaller groups

[45] Grylls, B. (2011). *Mud, Sweat and Tears.* Transworld Publishers, London. page 419. Used with permission under fair use guidelines of Penguin Random House

of Christians, meeting in neutral premises such as coffee shops, pubs, community halls, and homes.

Both of these expressions of church are serving the people. The first, the Cathedral or Mega church, serves mainly the need for individuals to connect with God. The church provides the "service" and the individuals come and listen and hopefully learn, discover, and connect with God. The second, the small group, mainly serves the need for individuals to connect to one another. The group provides opportunity to serve one another, to pray for one another, and to support and encourage one another. The problem is that these two expressions of church seem to be very different. The first is central and requires a massive building, a major organisational structure and significant funding, which in turn depends on the giving of the members of the congregation. The second requires very little of these things, but it does require the commitment of the members of the small group to come regularly and to actively serve each other.

Somehow we need to find a way to combine the best of both these expressions of church. The changes do not just need to be made in the Cathedral church and the Cafe church, the Mega church and the House Church, but also in the many small to mid-size churches, in towns all over the country, not big enough to have the draw of the Mega church experience, and not small enough to be the handful of believers supporting each other. These are the churches with which most Christian are familiar, the sort of church I have been leading for four decades: churches that, generally speaking, are declining in the UK. But there is great hope and I look forward to seeing how the church is going to wake up to the challenge of growing the faith that so many people do have, but is maybe as yet only in seed form. There are some ways in which I believe this can happen, by cultivating the soil to enable the seed to grow.

The place of the Sunday meeting

One of the most challenging issues we face as the church relates to our understanding of Sunday! For centuries, Sunday has been the "Day of Rest" for society and part of that "Day of Rest" has been attending church services. For its part, the church has been focussed around the Sunday meetings, usually two of them: morning and evening. When I was a child, there was "Sunday School" in the afternoon as well! Now we live in an increasingly seven day week society, where many people work on Sunday, in the service, care, leisure and retail industries, if not in manufacturing. For them Sunday may be part of the weekend, but it is hardly a "Day of Rest"!

This has caused a problem for church and a problem for society. The problem for church is that Sunday has been the main purpose of the organisation and the work of its leaders, whether they are paid ministers or volunteers. A new church leader is called usually for his or her ability to lead a Sunday service and preach a good sermon. But people are less and less inclined to come to a church meeting every Sunday, if at all. The problem for our society of the 24-7 way of life is illustrated by this summary from the Oxford University Nuffield Department of Clinical Sciences: *"We know that this imposed social structure is in conflict with our basic biology and suboptimal for our health"*.[46] A contributor to the Huffington Post, Susan Steinbrecher says, *"As leaders it is also good for the health of our employees if we take time to reconnect with ourselves and of course with the ones we love. A Kansas State University study shows that workers have a difficult time getting distance, mentally, from business matters if they stay connected beyond the workday— and therefore cannot move into a more relaxed state*

[46] www.ndcn.ox.ac.uk

during off-hours. We all need time for rest and renewal, and it is common sense that when we don't take that time, we become burned out and less effective—in all aspects of our lives".[47]

I believe we need to go back and think again about this "Day of Rest" or to give it the term the Bible uses, "The Sabbath". In Genesis chapter 3 we read that *"the man and his wife heard the sound of the Lord God as he was walking in the garden in the cool of the day"* (Genesis 3:8). I love the idea that Adam and Eve heard the sound of God walking in the garden—walking in a garden doesn't usually make a lot of noise! So what did they hear? Was it just footsteps, or was it perhaps the sound of singing? There is a beautiful reference in one of the later prophetic books of the Old Testament, Zephaniah, which tells us that when the Lord comes to restore the people, then *"He will take great delight in you; in his love he will no longer rebuke you, but will rejoice over you with singing"* (Zephaniah 3:17). I like to think that that was what God was doing in the

[47] Steinbrecher, S. (2014). *Why Our 24/7 Connected Society Is Driving Us Farther* Apart. [online] Huffington Post. Available at: http://www.huffingtonpost.com/susan-steinbrecher/why-our-247-connected-society-is-driving-us-farther-apart_b_5185925.html Accessed 28/09/2017

garden before we lost the relationship with him for which we were made. The "event" of Sabbath then for Adam and Eve was meeting with God, who was singing over them out of love; the Sabbath is for connecting with God.

In the New Testament we find Jesus going into the Synagogue on the Sabbath, *"as was his custom"* (Luke 4:16). The custom of Synagogue attendance grew in the years when the Jewish people were dispersed from their homeland, and were unable to focus on the temple celebrations in Jerusalem. But Jesus changed the whole Sabbath event! Luke tells us in chapter 4 that he read the words of the Old Testament prophet Isaiah; *"The Spirit of the Sovereign Lord is on me, because the Lord has anointed me to proclaim good news to the poor. He has sent me to bind up the broken hearted, to proclaim freedom for the captives and release from darkness for the prisoners, to proclaim the year of the Lord's favour"* (Isaiah 61:1-2: Luke 4:18-19). We noted earlier how this moment had a profound effect on the people: *"Then he rolled up the scroll, gave it to back to the attendant and sat down. The eyes of everyone in the synagogue were fastened on him."* (Luke 4:20). He began to explain that he was the person Isaiah was writing about and the "day" Isaiah had foretold had now come! That caused some stir! What mattered for Jesus was not that the people attended a meeting on the Sabbath, but that they met with the Lord!

As the Gospel unfolds we realise that Jesus is the Lord, he is God with us, and his presence is what we need, not necessarily a meeting in a building. Jesus made his position very clear when he said, *"The Sabbath was made for man, not man for the Sabbath"* (Mark 2:27). The purpose of the Sabbath was not for man to keep rules, but for man to be blessed by time spent with God. This is well illustrated when Jesus healed a man with a shrivelled hand on the Sabbath in the synagogue, and the Pharisees and Teachers of the law were *"furious"* (Luke 6:11). His words to the people on this occasion were, *"I ask you, which is lawful on the Sabbath: to do good or to do evil, to save life or to destroy it"* (Luke 6:9).

Paul made it clear that the followers of Jesus are no longer "under the law", which meant no longer obliged to follow the legalistic demands of the Jewish religion. When it comes to religious observance Paul wrote, *"Therefore do not let anyone judge you by what you eat or drink, or with regard to a religious festival, a New Moon celebration or a Sabbath day. These are a shadow of the things that were to come; the reality, however, is found in Christ"* (Colossians 2:16-17). That is Paul's one and only use of the term Sabbath. One would have thought that if observing the Sabbath in any form of institutional way was a vital part of the Christian life, then Paul would have said so and encouraged it. Instead he warns against setting up rules by which the Christians may be judged. The early church certainly met together, but at some point that moved from the Sabbath (our Saturday) to the First Day of the Week (our Sunday). For me, the issue is whether our Sunday has become too much a legalistic event that we have to attend, rather than one opportunity among many for us to meet together as believers to connect with God in a way that grows our faith.

When I began in ministry it was unthinkable that we might not have two services every Sunday, one at 11.00 am and one at 6.30 pm. Now it is quite rare to find such a pattern. If we go back to the Cathedral/Mega church model, there might indeed be two services, but there is more likely to be three or even four. For example, Hillsong in London has meetings every Sunday at 11.00 am, 1.15 pm, 4.00 pm, and 6.15 pm; whilst Canterbury Cathedral offers five different services, from 8.00 am Holy Communion to 6.30 pm Sermon and Compline. At the other end of the spectrum, Kahaila, a cafe-church in Brick Lane, London, meets every Wednesday evening; on Sundays they operate as a cafe engaging with the people who come to visit Brick Lane market.

There are some landmark churches, by which I mean they are setting a pattern which others are following, who have re-thought their Sunday programme. One such is St Thomas Philadelphia Church in Sheffield, which meets in small missional communities at various times both on Sundays and in the week, each community choosing the time that best suits its people and those to whom they are seeking to reach out. Every Sunday a number of those communities come together in a large place for a celebration gathering. On average it seems each small missional community joins a celebration like that two or three times a month.

Outside these larger or innovative churches the majority still persevere with Sunday morning at 11.00 (though more likely at 10 or 10.30!) and sometimes with an evening meeting as well. But this needs to change, and there are signs some churches are realising this. Churches are more willing to cancel meetings, to have different sorts of meetings and even to have, as my friend and evangelist Chris Duffet has suggested, "Sunday Out", when the church is encouraged to meet outside its buildings, maybe for a while in the town to meet people, or in their homes to gather for a meal. Rethinking Sunday needs to continue and develop.

Thinking back to the Sabbath of the Old Testament, it seems that the usual practice of Sabbath was within the extended family community. It was a household event rather than a larger one. But at festival times the whole community came together to celebrate their faith in the experiences of "Passover", "Weeks" and "Tabernacles". This twofold pattern of large gatherings at special times in the year, with more regular gatherings, extended household size, is something we need to explore. It ties in with what I said earlier about the balance between our individual faith and our celebrating together faith.

The Cathedral and Mega churches in our culture may in some way reflect the old tradition of festival worship, of the gathering of the whole community of believers. I can say with confidence that my own faith has been built up, it has grown, in the experience of large festival celebrations. I think back to the

Stoneleigh Bible weeks, to International conferences in Toronto, in Brighton and London, and to large joint church celebrations in Manchester, Bournemouth, Poole and Bedford. But equally the gathering together of a small group of believers has also been a fundamental part of my own growth in faith.

I think the answer for the many mid-size churches in towns and urban areas will be to concentrate their efforts into a large celebration meeting once or twice a month at most, perhaps joining with other Church groups in their town. Then, alongside these celebration meetings, they will provide meeting places and times for small groups of Christians, both on Sundays when the celebration is not happening and midweek, both daytime and evenings: in other words, a mixture of the celebration and the small group. But this will only be effective in keeping our faith growing if we make sure we understand both the place of worship and participation in these events.

Worship

In 2000 I had a break from my usual routine of work in order to take some time out for rest and renewal. Incidentally that sort of-break is called a "sabbatical": not a Saturday or Sunday, but an extended period of rest with the purpose of listening, learning, receiving and growing. I chose to visit a place where I had heard God was at work in a remarkable way.

There is a verse in the Old Testament in which the Prophet Zechariah assures the people that a time will come when members of all the nations will want to join in their faith: they will say, *"Let us go with you because we have heard that God is with you"* (Zechariah 8:23). I travelled to Canada, and went to a conference for pastors at the church in Toronto led by John and Carol Arnott. I was on the receiving end of much blessing during the visit. The greatest blessing was to rediscover that being a child of God is a sheer delight, and not a duty.

There was a song used at the conference written by Wayne Drain called *"Dancing with the Father"*.[48] The lyrics use a wonderful mixture of metaphors to describe God rescuing us, but the chorus describes how now, as children of God we can dance with the Father. And Wayne uses the image of a father throwing his child into the air and then putting him on his shoulders. Immediately I heard that, I was taken

[48] Drain, W. (1996). *Dancing with the Father.* Kingsway's ThankYou Music/MCPS

back to being a child, being swung between my parents as we walked along the promenade at Chalkwell Beach, and then being swung by my Dad up onto his shoulders where I felt so good! I discovered a verse in the Bible relating to this idea, and it has been a favourite of mine ever since. It is one of the blessings Moses speaks to the tribes of Israel before his death. *"About Benjamin he says, 'let the beloved of the Lord rest secure in him, for he shields him all day long, and the one the Lord loves rests between his shoulders'."* (Deuteronomy 33:12) One song led to a fresh awareness of who I am as a follower of Jesus and has continued to this day to inspire me. A very recent song recorded by Chris Tomlin among others, has had the same impact for many Christians. It is called *"Good Good Father"*.[49] It so simply communicates just how good our God is, and how loved we are by this good good heavenly father.

After the conference, I was able to go to a very remote and beautiful part of Canada, in an area of outstanding natural beauty called the Bruce Trail. I was staying in an isolated cabin on the shore of Lake Ontario. Whilst

[49] Brown, A.; Patrick, J and Barrett, M. (2014) *Good Good Father.* Lyrics ©Capitol Christian Music Group

reading my notes from the conference, I was reminded of a suggestion that was made for us to sit and write down the names of 100 people who had been a blessing to us in our lives so far. I thought at the time that might be difficult. But, by that lake, with no distractions other than the vast expanse of water in front of me, I found it both easy and delightful. The list went on and on, way beyond 100: people for whom I was grateful to God. Somehow people became more precious than ever that Sabbatical. My connection to God was renewed, cherished and made more intimate, and my connection to others made more genuine, grateful and wonderful.

All this came from worship. Books on the theme of worship have proliferated in the past few decades, most of them explaining in some way the two meanings of worship that we find in the Bible. The first, which is often expressed in the Psalms in the Old Testament, is the honouring of God with our coming together to sing, to bring our offerings, to pray and above all to praise. Psalm 95 is among the most quoted: *"Come, let us sing for joy to the Lord; let us shout aloud to the Rock of our salvation. Let us come before him with thanksgiving and extol him with music and song. For the Lord is the great God, the great King above all gods...Come, let us bow down in worship, let us kneel before the Lord our Maker; for he is our God and we are the people of his pasture, the flock under his care"* (Psalm 95:1-3,6-7). The second meaning of the word worship is more to do with honouring God with our lives, in the way we behave. It is found in verses such as, *"Therefore, I urge you, brothers and sisters, in view of God's mercy, to offer your bodies as a living sacrifice, holy and pleasing to God—this is your true and proper worship"* (Romans 12:1). To *"offer one's body as a living sacrifice"* means to seek to live our earthly lives in such a way that everything honours God who made us, and now has made us his own by our faith in Jesus. Eugene Peterson expresses this so well in his paraphrase of the verse: *"So here's what I want you to do, God helping you: Take your everyday, ordinary life—your sleeping, eating, going-to-work, and walking-around life—and place it before God as an offering"* (Romans 12:1 MSG).

Worship is the experience of personally and corporately expressing to God our faith and our love, and the way in which we conduct ourselves day by day. What joins these together for me is the sense of God with us, his holy presence! In a true sense, worship is connecting to God.

We are Easter people; resurrection is our beginning as well as our end. On Easter Day Jesus appeared *"when his disciples were together with the doors locked for fear of the Jewish leaders"* (John 20:19). His promise was both, *"Surely I am with you always, to the very end of the age"* (Matthew 28:20) and *"I am going to send you what my Father has promised"* (Luke 24:49), *"You will receive power when the Holy Spirit comes on you"* (Acts 1:8). Life was changed by his presence, both physically, when he appeared with them after Easter Sunday, and then in the presence of the Holy Spirit for all time in all believers.

Our lives need to be changed by his presence, and the heart of worship is being conscious that he is with us. We worry far too much about the content of our worship and not nearly enough about the context of our worship, which is the presence of the Risen Lord Jesus Christ!

Since leaving my full time leadership role I have had the opportunity to meet with Christians in a wide variety of settings, with different denominations and at different styles of service at various times of the week. In both Testaments, the Bible is clear that God is not confined to any time and space, to any building or to any ceremony. When King Solomon built the first temple in Jerusalem in the mid-10th Century BC, his dedication prayer recorded both in the books of Kings and the books of Chronicles included these words, *"But will God really dwell on earth? The heavens, even the highest heaven, cannot contain you. How much less this temple I have built!"* (1 Kings 8:27: 2 Chronicles 6:18). Although the community believed that they could meet with God in their temple, they also knew God was never to be limited to such a place.

Part of the learning curve of the exile, the period when the people were taken out of their homeland and forced to live in lands far away, was that God could be found wherever they were: *"Where can I go from your Spirit? Where can I flee from your presence? If I go up to the heavens, you are there; if I make my bed in the depths, you are there. If I rise on the wings of the dawn, if I settle on the far side of the sea, even there your hand will guide me, your right hand will hold me fast"* (Psalm 139:7-10). The New Testament makes the astounding claim that the followers of Jesus are now God's temple. Paul talked to the Christian believers in Ephesus, most of whom were not brought up in the Jewish family, but were Gentiles, and said to them: *"Consequently, you are no longer foreigners and strangers, but fellow citizens with God's people and also members of his household, built on the foundation of the apostles and prophets, with Christ Jesus himself as the chief cornerstone. In him the whole building is joined together and rises to become a holy temple in the Lord. And in him you too are being built together to become a dwelling in which God lives by his Spirit"* (Ephesians 2:19-22). God is not confined to any building made by human hands, because he chooses to come and meet with us who believe as we come together. Jesus said, *"For where two or three gather in my name, there am I with them"* (Matthew 18:20).

Worship is about recognising the presence of God with us. If we do that when we gather together, then we will be more able to maintain that awareness of God with us when we are on our own. And it is often when we are on our own that worship is our most powerful resource, when our response to circumstances we face is not dictated by our feelings but by his presence So back to our church meetings: different styles from very classical to very contemporary; different methods, from highly prepared to very spontaneous; different times, from a few minutes to a few hours, but what is essential if this meeting is to be true worship, is a conscious recognition of the presence of God. I have to say that I do not always discover that. Sometimes there is a nod to his presence at the start of a service, but then it is as if God is left in the back row as we get on with the service. Sometimes prayer is so quick (how we love the phrase *just a brief prayer*! As if we have to apologise for delaying our service for a moment to pray!), and so abrupt that I wonder if anyone realises that we are talking to the Lord who is with us. The focus of prayer should not be its length, or its eloquence, but a recognition of what we are doing: talking and listening to the present Lord.

The same goes for our songs. To stand up and sing a song and then move on to the next item on the service agenda so often to me seems to miss that this song is seeking to honour the Lord who is present with us. We should be far more conscious of the one to whom we are singing and respond to the songs with moments of wonder, maybe applause, maybe silence, but above all space to let God be with us.

When it comes to the preaching, I have been as guilty as anyone at mishandling the word of truth. Paul wrote to Timothy, *"Do your best to present yourself to God as one approved, a worker who does not need to be ashamed and who correctly handles the word of truth"* (2 Timothy 2:15). The issue is not so much how good the sermon is as to whether we are really aware that we are communicating God's Word, and that he is here with us. We need to make sure we have honoured Him in the sharing of this word. We are not the person who matters, Jesus is. We are simply spokespeople. Often on the news we will hear the newscaster say, "A spokesman for the family, or the government, or the president, said..." On television the spokesperson is there, but they are not named, they do not matter, it is the person for whom they speaking who matters. And when we preach we are speaking for Jesus: he matters, and people need to meet with him.

So my point is that we really do need to consider how at every point in our meeting together we are genuinely recognising the presence of God. If we do, there will be changes in what happens! I believe there will be more moments when people hear the Lord speaking to them, more moments of healing, more moments of freedom, more connecting to God. We will genuinely be practising the Sabbath. And for this to happen there is one other aspect of our connecting to God we need to consider, and that is our participation.

Participation

If you have ever attended a major outdoor event such as an agricultural show or a musical festival, you will recall how, as you approach the venue along the country road, there are signs directing you if you are a player or an exhibitor, and signs for a different entrance if you are a spectator. For a sporting event at the stadium, there is the players' entrance and there are the spectators' entrances. A theatre has its stage door for the performers and the foyer for the audience.

The church I attended as a child also had its front doors for the congregation and a back door for the important people! Our front doors led us to what was called "the vestibule" from which we moved into the "sanctuary" to take our seats. In front of us was a large raised platform with two doors, one on each side of a central pulpit raised even higher. The back door for the important people led to the rooms behind the pulpit and platform area. On Sunday, a group of men in their dark suits (they were all men in those days!) met before the meeting started in a room called the deacons' vestry. I always thought of it as like the staffroom at school! Then, just before the time for the service to begin, doors either side of the pulpit opened and these men filed out in line to take their seats. At the end of the line was the minister, who climbed the steps of the pulpit and led the meeting. It was very definitely 'them and us'! When it came to communion these men all filed back onto the platform and sat in a semi-circle around the minister, who was in the centre, and they prayed the prayers of thanksgiving before coming off the platform to serve the rest of us, who stayed in our seats, with bread and wine. Were we participants or spectators?

Paul wrote to the church at Corinth and said, *"Is not the cup of thanksgiving for which we give thanks a participation in the blood of Christ? And is not the bread that we break a participation in the body of Christ?"* (1 Corinthians 10:16). The word "participation" here is the Greek word "koinonia", which is difficult to translate into a single word. Other translations use the words, "fellowship", "communion" or "sharing", but the root of the word is "something which we have in common". Paul is saying that when we take bread together, breaking a piece off one loaf, and when we take some wine or juice together, all drinking out of one cup (or from little cups all poured from one bottle!), we are saying that we have in common our faith in Jesus as our Saviour.

We are all receiving the same grace of God, this undeserved love which has called us to believe in Jesus and now assures us of his mercy which has forgiven us and accepted us all as his children. Our participation in the bread and wine, the communion service, is saying that we share this faith together, and share equally in the grace God has given us to have such faith.

But when it comes to the practice of communion, and indeed the practice of church, it is all too easy to think of 'them and us', spectators who watch and listen and participants, those who are performing the event. The larger the crowd, the more acute this distinction becomes. When I attend a Cathedral service or a service at a Mega church, it is like watching artists on the stage. Of course, the fact that these events are now streamed on the internet makes it possible for people to watch them without even being there! It may be we are asked to participate, for example in singing, but it is my contention that if you are in a large audience at a worship service, the majority of the sound comes from the performers, especially when they are amplified by loudspeakers. I notice the sound of the people singing is quieter in these large congregations than in smaller congregations. In fact, the smaller the audience is, the more the audience becomes the participants. For example, when we meet in a home, just a few of us, there is no 'them and us' because we are all participating.

Now the issue for me is this: is Paul's call for us to "participate" in the body and blood of Christ sufficiently explained by the truth that we all share the same common faith, expressed in our being at the communion service, or is there more to this? Is there a truth that in the "Body of Christ", which is all believers, we are all to take part in the life of that Body?

I think back to my experience as child of the Sunday Service, with the audience sitting in their rows of pews and the leaders sitting on the platform at the front. Then I think of the event which we as children went out to, whilst the preacher preached! As I have mentioned already it was called "Children's Own", and the essence of this meeting was that we, the audience, were the participants. We all played a part: we played the piano, we read from the Bible, we told the Bible stories, we prayed, we sang. I thank God for that meeting, and for the inspiring lady behind it. It set into my mind that we need to make church something in which everyone genuinely participates.

In his letter to the church at Corinth, Paul goes on from talking about our participation in the body and blood of Christ to talk about spiritual gifts. He says, *"Now to each one the manifestation of the Spirit is given for the common good"* (1 Corinthians 12:7). A little further on he adds, *"Now you are the body of Christ and each one is a part of it"* (1 Corinthians 12:27), and then, *"What then shall we say brothers and sisters? When you come together each of you has a hymn, or a word of instruction, a revelation, a tongue or an interpretation"* (1 Corinthians 14:26).What does it mean for each of us to have a part, to participate? Is Paul thinking only of a Sunday meeting? He does not say this refers to such a specific event, he simply says, *"when you come together."* Maybe Paul is thinking more of the life of the Body of Christ worked out day by day, through the worship of the people, BOTH their meetings of praise and sharing the word, AND their lives with each other and in their community? The gifts of the Holy Spirit include serving, encouraging, giving, showing mercy and hospitality (Romans 12:7-8, 13). These are aspects of Christian living wholly relevant to everyday and not just a Sunday meeting.

Surely the answer is that every believer, everyone who has this faith which joins them to Jesus, has a part to play in this amazing reality of the Body of Christ, which we think of as the church. Anything which suggests a "them and us" mentality, players and spectators, participants and audience, is contrary to the way the Bible shows us. So it is important to find ways in which everyone connects to one another when we come together. There needs to be room for testimony and prayer and words of encouragement shared by the people who are present, and there needs to be opportunities to serve one another in listening, praying, sharing words of wisdom and practical support. If we have the mentality that everyone is a participant then there will be ways to make this participation reality; if we have the mentality that church leaders are 'doing' the event and we are there just to watch, then that is all it will be. We will leave assessing their performance rather than amazed at His presence with us.

It would be remiss of me to write these pages without mentioning one Christian who has helped me in so many ways for the past three decades. He is John Piper, a prolific writer, whose books I have greatly appreciated. One which stands out and I commend to other ministers is *"Brothers, We Are Not Professionals"*. My 2002 edition is the original, but in 2013 a new edition with extra chapters was published. The essence of the book is to remind those of us in ministry that the church is not just another professional organisation of which we are the managers. It is God's people, and we are utterly dependent upon Him for everything in that church. Whenever we preach or pastor people we do so as servants of Jesus, needing his grace and power for each situation. If we rely on our professionalism, our education, our skill or our experience we are likely to fail. If we continue to humbly recognise our need before the Lord we may just be effective for him.

Here are two telling quotations: *"We Pastors are being killed by the professionalizing of the pastoral ministry"*, *"God is not looking for people to work for Him but people who let Him work mightily in and through them"*.[50] These statements apply to all of us as Christians, not just church leaders. Many miracles happen through the participation of believers in the sharing of God's love with people they know and encounter in their daily lives. But the truth is more miracles can happen if we allow our faith to grow. God

[50] Piper, J. (2002/2013). *Brothers, We Are Not Professionals: A Plea to Pastors for Radical Ministry.* Nashville: Broadman & Holman Publishers. Permission requested

will use each of us mightily in the service of His kingdom.

This book has been all about growing the faith of our people. Faith is that living relationship we have with God through Jesus, by his Spirit, which impacts our lives all the time. The purpose of growing faith is to make our lives fruitful for Jesus. A portion of Jesus' own words carries this message vividly: *"I am the vine, you are the branches. If you remain in me and I in you, you will bear much fruit; apart from me you can do nothing"* (John 15:5). Jesus is not only talking to leaders here, or to special people; we all belong to His vine. There are no independent branches. An independent branch is a dead branch. If we are all to be fruit bearing branches of the vine, all of us need to play a part in the "faith-sharing" of the church.

Anything which suggests otherwise is to be challenged. I challenge the way that so often I have operated! By thinking that someone is "good" at leading services, at praying in a meeting, at preaching, it is very easy to suggest that others are not good enough. Earlier this year I attended a service in quite a large congregation. After some songs, the leader stood up to say something when another person in the congregation began to pray. The prayer was passionate and encouraging. When he had finished, the leader said, "That was a much better prayer than the one I was going to pray!" He followed up the theme of the prayer, encouraging us to receive what had been prayed for. What was spoken by the unknown member of that congregation may not have been the most eloquent prayer, the most economic use of words, but it spoke to God, and God spoke to us and it was a good moment. When I hear our prepared prayers and prepared sermons I do wonder sometimes if we are not quenching the Spirit who would be speaking through others if we let Him.

Of course there is a gift of preaching and teaching. But if that becomes so central that others feel they are spectators we have missed the point. Here's another of Jesus' teachings to think about: *"The student is not above the teacher, but everyone who is fully trained will be like their teacher"* (Luke 6:40). We have a mandate to teach others so that they can teach others. Paul says, *"The one who receives instruction in the word should share all good things with their instructor"* (Galatians 6:6). If trained preachers are the only ones who speak, how are we being true to the genuine participation of all?

Nadia Bolz-Weber writing in her book *"Cranky Beautiful Faith"*, speaks of the church she sought to lead like this: *"Ours was not a church where you passively consume some sort of religious product produced for you based on market research. We were a DIY Church; we made art and sang acapella, most of the liturgy was led by whoever wanted to lead it that week and we sat in the round"*.[51]

Mike Yakonelli wrote his book *"Messy Spirituality"* to share some of his experience of church where very ordinary, and often very messy, people belonged. He told stories of people participating who were far from perfect, but whose very imperfection spoke volumes about the grace of God which accepts us. He said himself of the book: *"Messy Spirituality" has the audacity to suggest that messiness is the workshop of faith, the greenhouse of authentic spirituality – the place where Jesus meets the real us"*.[52]

Our connections together as believers are vital to our growth: meeting together for worship recognises the

[51] Bolz-Weber, N. (2013). *Cranky Beautiful Faith: For irregular (and regular) people*. Canterbury Press. Used with permission

[52] Yakonelli, M. (2001), *Messy Spirituality: Christianity for the rest of us*. Hodder and Stoughton. Permission requested

presence of Jesus with us, our participation in the life of the community and serving one another with the gifts of the Holy Spirit. But we are also called to connect to those who as yet do not share our faith.

Evangelism

God loves this world. Putting that into the present tense strikes me more powerfully than the past tense of *"God so loved the world that he gave his one and only Son"* (John 3:16). This Bible text has probably been used more than any other to tell the story of Jesus, and of course it remains a great word. But it is possible to hear it and take the attitude, "God may have loved the world then, but what about me, living my life in the 21st century?". Chris Duffet, founder of the Light Project describes evangelism like this: *"To do evangelism is to connect with others in a big hearted way showing a big hearted God"*.[53] The single most important method Chris employs to connect with others is to show them and tell them that God loves them.

[53] www.lightproject.org.uk
Duffet, C. and Goddard, S. (2012). *Big Hearted*. Gilead Books Publishing. Used with permission

If we think of the growth of the Christian faith in the book of Acts, we are likely to associate evangelism with the events of the day of Pentecost, when Peter stood up and boldly proclaimed the message about Jesus, prompting three thousand people to become believers on that one day. We are less likely to immediately think of the time Paul went down to the riverside with Luke, the writer of the story and the travelling companion of Paul. Luke writes, *"We sat down and began to speak to the women who had gathered there"* (Acts 16:13). Paul and Luke, a couple of men, on the Jewish Sabbath, sat down and talked with a group of women; this is not so unlikely today, but surely not to be expected in those days. Yet Luke tells us that, as the women listened, one of them, a lady called Lydia, became curious about what Paul was saying. She had faith in God, but as yet knew nothing of Jesus. As Paul spoke, the Holy Spirit *"opened her heart to respond to Paul's message"* (Acts 16:14), and she and her household became believers.

Here are two models for evangelism in the book of Acts: Peter preaching to crowds and Paul sitting down with a handful. Which model of evangelism has the church copied, preaching to thousands or sitting down with just one non-believer? When I began in ministry the answer was definitely the first model: the preaching of the Gospel by an evangelist to a crowd, Billy Graham style. But over the years the other model has been slowly gathering momentum. I say slowly, because it has been slow. Today, people still hanker after the big evangelistic event, and as I write preparations are being made for such an event at one of the Premier Football League stadia in the UK, the Emirates, home of Arsenal football club. Premier Radio reports that, *"The 'JustOne Emirates' event is scheduled to take place on 8 July 2017 and is expected to cost £750,000."* Speaking to Premier Radio, Canon J John who is hosting the event said: *"Five years ago I felt the Lord say, 'It's time to proclaim the good news of Jesus Christ in the football stadiums'. They are the secular cathedrals. To fill a stadium like the Emirates says something. There are millions of people in London who have never been to church. They might come to the Emirates and that might be a stepping stone to them walking nearer to Jesus".*[54] J John is quick to say that such an event is not the answer to bringing revival in London, but he hopes it may be a "tipping point" that leads to change. I can only share his hope, and pray for that event. And yet all the time, all the days before

[54] www.premier.org.uk 8th October 2015

that event and all the days after that event, there are possibilities of people like Lydia, who we can meet by the riverside, the school gates, the coffee shop or the market square, willing to hear the message about Jesus. There are probably far more like this than we have ever imagined, those whose hearts God may yet open to the truth of Jesus. But it calls for people like me and you to be willing to go to the riverside and sit with them.

As I think back over the many years the church has been trying to do evangelism, I honestly believe that two things are pretty clear. The first is that we have made more connections with un-churched people through a wide range of non-Sunday, non-service events such as Alpha and Mother and toddler groups than we have ever made by specific Sunday evangelistic meetings. The second is that the process by which people have come to faith has largely involved friendships made with one or more of the Christians in our church. Many years ago, a lady in our church whose husband was not a Christian, asked me if I might consider playing a game of golf with him. Now I was very poor at golf and I was concerned it would be an utter fiasco. But I did ask him, and we did play that first game. We continued to play golf together for years, often starting very early in the morning to fit the game into our busy schedules. Little by little our friendship grew, as did the sharing of our lives. Alan worked as a manager in hospital engineering and, when our church was planning a trip to Romania (post the 1989 revolution in that country) to take medical aid, Alan was invited to join the trip. As usually happened on such a trip, we went to a church service, and Alan came and was introduced. But then he was asked by the Romanian Pastor to say a few words. He stood up and, to our amazement, spoke of how he had come to believe in Jesus. He is now serving as a church Elder. The connection we had made with him had led to his heart being opened to the Lord.

The secret of Alpha is that it develops connections with people. Either people are invited as friends of one of the believers, or if they turn up on their own accord at Alpha, they find themselves accepted and befriended in a genuine way. They are not just befriended in order that they might become a Christian, but befriended in a way that believers seek to come alongside them, listen to them, accept them as they are, support them and share in their lives just out of love for them. But what about the people who do not have church friends, or who will not come to a church based group? Paul went and found Lydia by the riverside.

In his first book, *"Smack Heads and Fat Cats"*, Chris Duffet writes about a group of drug addicts he met on the tow path of a canal, "by the riverside". One day he came to meet them and found a guy there, whose name was Simon. He was in a particularly bad way, having probably taken some "bad" drugs. The others were leaving, but Chris felt he had to stay. He writes, *"I simply knew that I should pray for Simon. I didn't tell him, or anyone else for that matter, I just prayed quietly and laid my hand on his shoulder. After a few seconds, Simon turned to me and said, 'That's it Chris, the hand of God'".*[55] The result was nothing short of dramatic, both in the physical healing the man experienced and his subsequent change of heart. The challenge to us is to find ways to get alongside people who are "by the riverside." They may be people we just happen to be next to in a queue or on a bus, train or plane.

But there can be a more intentional way to connect with people. Chris has encouraged the church to get

[55] Duffet, C. (2009). *Smack Heads and Fat Cats*. Gilead Books Publishing. Used with permission

out of the building and be what he called "saints on the street": going out as team to meet people, to offer them coffee and cake, water on a hot day, soup on a cold day, to offer the opportunity to pray for healing, or just to be there to listen. I personally found listening a great way of connecting, so I dedicated some of my time to sitting in a particular coffee shop in town and looking for someone with whom to engage in conversation.

The reality we discover is that we can get alongside others. As we listen to the Spirit of God we will discover that he will provide opportunity to share the truth with others, to pray with them, and maybe see their lives opening to Jesus. However, the most fundamental necessity in all this is to remember that we set out to love the people. If God so loved the world that he gave, then we too need to love the world as we go. "Loving the people" means taking time to be with them and to take an interest in them. That sort of involvement is costly, in time and in energy. If we are expected to do that, and to maintain a host of structured programmed events at the church base, we will quickly wear out. The truth is that we, institutional church, have worn many out! The real question we need to ask is whether or not what we are doing as a church is genuinely providing opportunities to come alongside and have time for people. I believe that as we realise God wants to use all of us to connect with (as yet) unbelievers, our whole concept of evangelism will shift from being a church-based event to an everyday lifestyle.

Just as we need to connect with God in a personal relationship of faith, and just as church is about connecting to one another to be together in his presence and honour Him with our worship, so evangelism is about connecting to people so that they might discover the presence of God. If, as I said earlier, *"Blessing is God's presence on the move"*, then wherever we go we are to bring blessing to others.

Peter's letter in the New Testament has some very powerful words for us about this. He writes, *"In your hearts revere Christ as Lord. Always be prepared to give an answer to everyone who asks you to give the reason for the hope that you have. But do this with gentleness and respect"* (1 Peter 3:15). Peter was writing to Christians who were under pressure, being laughed at perhaps, mocked or even threatened for their faith, and yet continued to live with hope. We are more often ignored than mocked, and yet inwardly we can feel that nobody wants to hear our message, nobody cares about Christianity anymore; there is too much scandal in the church for us to say anything. And yet if we live with hope in our hearts whatever the circumstances, then we will find people wondering why we are able to cope in the way we do. And of course the reason is our faith. That is what we need to grow within us so it produces the fruit of lives of faith, which in turn can bless other people.

Another very powerful word from Peter's letter is this: *"Do not repay evil with evil or insult with insult. On the contrary, repay evil with blessing, because to this you were called so that you may inherit a blessing"* (1 Peter 3:9). You have probably heard of the expression "pay it forwards." The idea is that one day you may need a good deed done to you, so you do a good deed to someone now, as payment in advance for what you will receive one day! It was popularised by the 2000 film of that name. But Peter gives us a far greater challenge here. He invites us *"to pay back evil with blessing."* Wherever we are on the receiving end of something that is unkind, or unfair, or malicious, we pay back, not with revenge or anger or retaliation, but with blessing. Jesus said, *"Love your enemies, do good to those who hate you, bless those who curse you, pray for those who mistreat you"* (Luke 6:27-28). If we could take these principles and set out each day to live by them, we just might see people's lives opening up to Jesus. Blessing other people is more than just saying "God bless you", though it may well include saying that! It is about being willing to respond to a need when we see it, to add light into darkness where we encounter it, and to bring comfort and peace to distress when we enter it.

A great example of how God works through the friendships we offer is the life of a man called Gonville Ffrench-Beytagh (1912-1991). His multi-cultural background included China, where he began his life, England, where he spent his childhood, New Zealand, the site of his teenage years, and South Africa, where he went to work. The latter was where he became attracted to Christianity by "the example of friends", and from his early days as a believer felt called into the priesthood. In his role as a church leader, he challenged much of the establishment and was arrested, tried, and convicted because of his anti-apartheid activities. After his release from prison he came back to England and spent the rest of his years blessing many through his teaching.

His book, *"Encountering Light"*, came into my hands soon after I began my ministry and I have kept that copy ever since. So much of what is in that book resonates with the themes I have been exploring here. His chapter on *"the company of the beloved"* (his name for the church) is so relevant, even though the book is now over 40 years old. I love this section: *"One thing I am sure about. If we Christians really believed in the love and forgiveness of God which we proclaim so glibly, our churches would be much odder, madder and more joyful places than they are now".*[56]

He goes on to talk about the call for Jesus' followers to go and make disciples. He talks of the "danger" of committing ourselves to God, but offers the thought that, in a world where we try to shield ourselves and our children from danger, we actually need some outlet for risk in our lives—something of the adventure for which we were made. He suggests we might find this adventure by taking the love of God out wherever we go. He ends his book like this: *"The question always is 'how do I follow Christ, here where I am? How can the Lord, the Spirit, work in this place to make men and women more whole? How can love grow here in this factory, this home, this office, school?' And*

[56] Ffrench-Beytagh, G. (1975) *Encountering Light*. Fontana. Permission requested

because we are unique, because there is no one who can take our particular place in creation, if you or I do not find the answer and act upon it, nobody will".[57]

For me, bringing blessing wherever I go is the real challenge. And it takes me right back to the first part of this book, to conversation. The more I am aware of a conversation with God, the more it is possible to receive and give the blessing of God. I might hear a news item of tragedy, and my first thought is to lift the situation to my heavenly Father that he might bless it, that goodness will flood in where evil has so clearly been at work. I may be prompted to give something into that situation. I might see someone walking down the road looking "weary worn and sad" and I ask God to bless them. I may be prompted to greet that person and offer them, at the very least, a human smile. I might encounter an argument, and I quietly seek that God's peace comes to rule. Blessing, seeking God's immediate presence, becomes my default reaction. Oh would that this were always the case! But I thank God for the little I have learned and felt of its amazing power.

[57] Ibid.

So where does this lead us? The evangelist J. John, writing in his meditations for Holy Week 2016, comments on Jesus' words spoken when he was dying on the cross. He said to his mother, *"Woman here is your son"* and to the disciple, his friend John, *"Here is your mother"* (John 19:26-27). The way he spoke to his mother was not at all disrespectful; the word "woman" implies much more the sense of "Dear Lady". J John writes: *"What we see here is something that is present throughout the Gospels. Jesus saw his purpose not just to forgive people as individuals but to create through them a new community – a people who would be based not on racial or family ties, but on their relationship to him through faith".*[58] The church is something so utterly different from any other grouping of people in this world. It really is unique, in the true sense that Jesus is the unique Son of God.

As a family of people brought together entirely by faith in Jesus, and not by our own past or present lives, the church challenges so much of the world's ideology. J John says: *"Our Western culture emphasises the individual over everything else. Here, Jesus looks away from himself to show both care for family and his*

---

[58] John J (2015) *It is finished* Philo Trust. Used with permission

commitment to the Christian community. We need to practise this too".[59] Just as Jesus needed his friends as he faced his death, just as he joined Mary and John together as a sign on the new community, so the resurrection connected people together as they shared their faith that their Jesus was and is alive. *"Spiritual formation",* another way of speaking of growing in faith, is, according to Eugene Peterson, *"something which happens in the company of friends".*[60]

Our conversation with God, and our curiosity about Him and all He is saying and doing are ways through which we will keep our faith growing. In the same way, so are our connections to other people, and our doing and being church in a way that always is defined by the presence of Jesus with us.

[59] Ibid.
[60] Peterson, E. (2006). *Living The Resurrection.* Navpress. Used with permission

Chapter 4

Measuring Faith Growth

Writing these pages has reminded me of much that God has spoken into my life over many years. Looking back, I can see how there has been a continued growing of faith as I have sought to keep listening to God and talking with him, as I have kept on being curious, reading books, listening to others, looking at this world around us, and as I have made connections with the wonderful people God has put around me. Among my treasures are photo albums given to me by the communities I have served, containing pictures of some of the people with whom I have journeyed. They remind me of the pleasure of being in the company of fellow believers, and I shall keep looking at them as long as I live. Faith has grown, but is this growth something we can measure?

People like to measure things! The academic world calls this "Statistics". When it comes to church growth there is a great deal of statistical information available. The Church of England has its own research unit: their web site, begins like this. "*Welcome to the statistics pages. Here, you will be able to find key statistics and trends in relation to church growth and decline of the Church of England. Data has been provided by the Archbishops' Council".[61]*

Statistics are fascinating for some people! I have a publication from the National Physics Laboratory in London called *"The little big book of metrology"* It explains the great precision with which scientists define their measurements. For example, a metre is defined as, *"the length of the path travelled by light in vacuum during a time interval of 1/299,792,458 of a second".[62]* Sometimes it has seemed that we want to go to the same lengths to measure church growth, or, as in the current state of affairs in the UK church, the church's decline.

I love a picture painted in the book of Zechariah in the Old Testament. The prophet sees a man with a tape measure in his hand and asks him where he is going. The man replies that he is going to measure the dimensions of the city walls of Jerusalem.

[61] www.churchgrowthresearch.org.uk
There are similar statistics available from the Evangelical Alliance, and from www.faithsurvey.co.uk
[62] National Physics Laboratory, 2008

Immediately, a messenger from heaven is dispatched to run and tell the man with tape measure, *"Jerusalem will be a city without walls because of the great number of people and animals in it. And I myself will be a wall of fire around it,' declares the Lord, 'and I will be its glory within'"* (Zechariah 2:4-5). Spiritual things cannot be measured with human dimensions!

In the book of Revelation, the measurements of the City of God are given as a perfect cube. The angel sent to explain the vision of the new heaven and the new earth to John has a rod in his hand with which to measure the city's dimensions. The rod was a standard of measuring in ancient days, and was about 5 metres in length. The results were that the city's walls were each 12,000 stadia—length, breadth and height! 12,000 stadia is about 2,200 kilometres or 1400 miles (Revelation 21:15-16).

I quite often travel to Timisoara which is on the west side of Romania, about 2,200 kilometres from where I live in England. It takes about three hours flying time to get there, or 2 full days driving. Imagine walking there and stopping every 5 metres to measure! How on earth do you measure 2,200 kilometres of a vertical wall? These are not to be taken as literal human dimensions: the point is that God's city will be perfect. 12 is the number of completeness in the book of Revelation; just as there were twelve tribes of Israel and twelve disciples of Jesus, so the final city of God will be perfect in every way.

We may try to use human measurements for church growth, but when it comes to faith growth and spiritual growth we need another way of measuring. Paul writes about this in his letter to the Ephesians. He speaks about the ministries of church, *"the apostles, the prophets, the evangelists, the pastors and teachers"*, and says that their purpose is *" that the body of Christ may be built up until we all reach unity in the faith and in the knowledge of the Son of God and become mature, attaining to the whole measure of the fullness of Christ"* (Ephesians 4:12-13). He offers the same idea when he prays for his friends in these words: *"I pray that you, being rooted and established in love, may have power, together with all the Lord's holy people, to grasp how wide and long and high and deep is the love of Christ, and to know this love that surpasses knowledge – that you may be filled to the measure of all the fullness of God"* (Ephesians 3:17-19). Just as God's love cannot be measured in human statistics, neither can our faith which is about the presence of Christ in us, filling us *"to the measure of the fullness of God"* with his love. Complete growth is to reach *"the whole measure of the fullness of Christ."* So the question remains, how do we measure that? If not by statistics, what other means do we have to see that faith is growing?

Jesus told a simple story: *"This is what the kingdom of God is like. A man scatters seed on the ground. Night and day, whether he sleeps or gets up, the seed sprouts and grows, though he does not know how. All by itself the soil produces corn – first the stalk, then the ear, then the full grain in the ear. As soon as the corn is ripe, he puts the sickle to it, because the harvest has come"* (Mark 4:26-29). The growth of the seed is something that happens and little by little you notice it. First a little green sprout emerges, then a long stalk with leaves and then the seed-bearing ear of corn ready to be harvested. In another image, Jesus spoke of the growth when he said, *"by their fruit you will recognise them"* (Matthew 7:20). There will be something clearly observable in the lives of those whose faith is growing, and I think we can see this in two ways. Firstly, we will see more and more of what Paul calls *"the fullness of God"*, the nature of God's character of goodness. Secondly, we will see how God works in his people to produce good fruit.

Being aware of the goodness of God

In 1992 I took time to go back to my roots, to the places of my childhood: Thundersley, Leigh on Sea and Southend on Sea. I went to my childhood playground, Leigh cliffs, the Old Leigh cockle sheds and what was then called Two Tree Island. Nowadays it is One Tree Island as the other was struck by lightning! I peered in through the railings of my old school, and I walked along the pier, smiling at my early childhood ambition to be a pier train driver!

The word from God that so strongly affected me at that time was about his goodness: *"You are good and what you do is good."* (Psalm 119:68). It was challenging to look back over my life and remember things that had not always been good. My schooldays had been spoilt in part by bullying, my mother died when I was only seventeen and the family had been somewhat scattered as a result, leaving us very much on our own. But there was a clear strand of goodness running through all of life, even through those difficult experiences. I found a book which was helpful in sharpening my sense of the goodness of God. It was written by Robert Schuller, an American Pastor of a Mega church in California. His building was called the Grove Cathedral and was nicknamed the Crystal

Cathedral, being an early example of a building clad almost entirely in glass panels. There was something very brash and indulgent about the whole thing, such a contrast to Jesus walking the hills with his band of followers, picking ears of corn from the side of the fields, and telling his friends not to worry about what to eat or wear. The book was titled, *"Life's Not Fair, But God Is Good".* It is very dated now and Dr Schuller died in 2015, but at the time the book made me think and grow in my faith in the goodness of God. Robert Schuller wrote, *"Life is unfair, but don't blame God. God is good. Let God in and he will show you that goodness works. Life's not fair but don't confuse life with God".*[63]

As I explored this idea I began to discover more of the richness of the goodness of God. The Psalms became more meaningful than ever before—these songs of praise and prayer connect us to God in a powerful way. I remember coming back and preaching from these words: *"I remain confident of this: I will see the goodness of the Lord in the land of the living. Wait for the Lord; be strong and take heart and wait for the Lord"* (Psalm 27:13-14). The words seemed to have an

[63] Schuller, R. H. (1991). *Life's Not Fair But God Is Good: How to Turn Life's Challenges Into Triumphs.* Bantam. Permission requested

impact. People spoke to me about their faith being strengthened, and one lady in particular reminded me for years afterwards about this message which had so affected her.

At that time I can honestly say that I gained a taste for the Lord's goodness. This idea comes from, *"Taste and see that the Lord is good"* (Psalm 34:8). Tasting is one of our biological senses, one we all too easily take for granted until we lose it! A UK charity working to help people suffering from smell and taste-related disorders writes: *"Smell and taste disorders have been shown to have a major impact on the quality of life of those affected".*[64] Most of us have favourite foods, things we just love to taste. My wife loves liquorice, the saltier the better, and even more so if it comes from Germany! That's not to my liking: I prefer Turkish delight, and that's even better when it comes from Turkey! God's goodness comes from God, so to be with God, to talk with God, to listen to God and to connect with his people is to be infected by goodness—to keep tasting his goodness, goodness

---

[64] Fifthsense.org, (2014). *The Impact of Smell and Taste Disorders.* [online]. Available at: http://www.fifthsense.org.uk/the-impact-of-smell-and-taste-disorders/ Accessed 02/10/2017

that never fails. It is interesting to note that our tastes can change!

It is possible that we begin with a taste for the goodness of God but then gradually, if we do not appreciate this quality of goodness, we begin to think more of other tastes. If we lose the sense of the goodness of God we are liable to a reduction in spiritual quality of life and to spiritual depression, feeling that God has forgotten us.

The greater our taste for God's goodness, the more we can trust that God will work *"for good"* in our lives. The verse from which this phrase *"for good"* comes is in Paul's Romans letter: *"And we know that in all things God works for the good of those who love him, who have been called according to his purpose"* (Romans 8:28). It takes faith to see that the goodness of God means that if we ask God into our lives, then whatever happens to us, however bad it may appear, the circumstances will be affected by the goodness of God. The goodness of God will be at work in ways we often will not see at the time, but we can trust that it is happening. It is one thing to know the words of Romans 8:28, it is another thing to hear them as God speaking to us in the darkness and pain of our situation, and then finding we have the faith to trust these words completely. How strong that faith is will depend on how confident we are of the goodness of God. So being aware of the goodness of God is vital to us.

It is like the gardener seeing on the front of a seed packet the picture of beautiful flowers or luscious fruit, and trusting that the seed can grow into these final results. The more we are aware of the goodness of God the more we can trust that God is growing us to be like that! If we were to put a picture on the seed packet of faith it would be of Jesus. An old brother who I still meet at the church where I began my ministry is right—the seed is to grow in us so we become like Jesus. I used to sing it as a child, *"Like Jesus, like Jesus, I want to be like Jesus; I love him so I want to grow like Jesus every day".*[65]

But what does that really mean? It isn't to be the same person as Jesus. We all celebrate our different personalities and gifts and appearances, each of us is individually unique to our Maker. Max Lucado made that wonderfully clear in his classic children's book, *"You Are Special"*. That will forever remain for me a

[65] Fanny J Crosby (1820-1915) who wrote this under one of her very many pseudonyms, Ida S Taylor

story worth telling with its climactic conversation between the Carpenter Eli and one of his creations, Punchinello. Punchinello has gone to see the Carpenter, his maker. Punchinello is so aware of his failings; the others in his community—called Wemmicks—have made that only too clear to him as well. The conversation between the carpenter and Punchinello goes like this:

"Oh, you don't have to defend yourself to me, child. I don't care what the other Wemmicks think."

"You don't?"

"No, and you shouldn't either. Who are they to give stars or dots? They're Wemmicks just like you. What they think doesn't matter, Punchinello. All that matters is what I think. And I think you are pretty special."

Punchinello laughed. "Me, special? Why? I can't walk fast. I can't jump. My paint is peeling. Why do I matter to you?"

Eli looked at Punchinello, put his hands on those small wooden shoulders, and spoke very slowly. "Because you're mine. That's why you matter to me".[66]

We are not to become identical clones, but we are to become like Jesus as the goodness of God, the fullness of Christ, deeply affects us, so that who we are and how we live displays this goodness to the world around us. So one measure of our faith growth is how strong a taste we have for the goodness of God. The other is something others will notice: the fruit that comes from the goodness of God at work in us.

Displaying good fruit

I love the Bible's message that God's people are somehow "on display". This is not the sort of display that celebrities seek, in the spotlight, on TV, or on the front page, on the contrary this is about being very ordinary people, living humble lives, and yet people seeing in us the goodness of God. John the Baptist is described by John, the fisherman follower of Jesus, like this: *"There was a man sent from God whose name*

---

[66] Lucado, M. (2000). Taken from *You are Special* by Max Lucado, © 1993, 1997, 2002, pp. 25-26. Used by permission of Crossway, a publishing ministry of Good News Publishers, Wheaton, IL 60187, ww.crossway.org.

was John. He came as a witness to testify concerning that light, so that through him all might believe. He himself was not the light; he came only as a witness to the light". (John 1:6-8).

We are to be witnesses of Jesus, in the sense that as people see us and our lives, they are going to see the goodness of God! Isaiah received this word from the Lord: *"You are my servant, Israel, in whom I will display my splendour"* (Isaiah 49:3). We are to fulfil that word in our day and age, to be witnesses who display the goodness of God, the fullness of Christ, as the Holy Spirit works in our lives.

Another way of describing this display of the fullness of Christ is to talk about fruit: the good fruit of God which will develop as we grow in our faith. Jesus said, *"Make a tree good and its fruit will be good, or make a tree bad and its fruit will be bad, for a tree is recognised by its fruit"* (Matthew 12:33). In his second letter in the New Testament, Peter encourages his fellow believers to keep growing: he says that *"if you possess these qualities in increasing measure, they will keep you from being ineffective and unproductive in your knowledge of our Lord Jesus Christ"* (2 Peter 1:8). The key thought here is that there is something to be seen as our faith increases.

A friend of mine sent me an e-mail in which he wrote, *"Our faith continues to be tested as we face new challenges and work pressures, but we know that God will look after us and he provides, not always what we want but what we need."* His Christian faith has been growing in the few years I have known him, and as I watch him and his family face some grave difficulties in their lives, I see someone whose faith is increasing and producing fruit. Faith will visibly grow when it is tested, through the situations of life which frustrate and disturb and limit our lives. If in those times we find ourselves talking more with God, asking questions like Job and drawing strength from the connections we have with other believers, then we can be sure that our faith is increasing. If in those times we find ourselves ignoring God, becoming bitter rather than curious and withdrawing from the connections with God's people, then that is a sign of a faith that is not growing.

Peter was very aware of the gift of his faith. He was a companion of Jesus for three years but at the time of Jesus' greatest need, when he had been arrested and was taken for trial, Peter denied he even knew Jesus. Yet Jesus never disowned Peter, and after the resurrection he came to Peter to offer him again his hand of welcome. The words Peter wrote in his first letter are in one sense his own story: *"Praise be to the God and Father of our Lord Jesus Christ! In his great mercy he has given us new birth into a living hope through the resurrection of Jesus Christ from the dead"* (1 Peter 1:3).

Peter recognised the immense value of this gift of faith, and said so at the start of his second letter. He writes, *"To those who through the righteousness of our God and Saviour Jesus Christ have received a faith as precious as ours"* (2 Peter 1:1). Then he goes on to urge his friends, his fellow believers, to grow in their faith. He says, *"Make every effort to add to your faith goodness; and to goodness, knowledge; and to knowledge, self-control; and to self-control, perseverance; and to perseverance, godliness; and to godliness, mutual affection; and to mutual affection, love. For if you possess these qualities in increasing measure, they will keep you from being ineffective and unproductive in your knowledge of our Lord Jesus Christ"* (2 Peter 1:5-8). The idea here is not that faith is insufficient for our salvation, and that we need to add other things to it, but that our faith, in order to keep growing, needs the nutrients of a healthy growing medium, just as seeds need the nutrients in a good soil. And the list Peter gives are the sort of qualities which will grow as we converse with God and wonder at his goodness and love, as we keep on being curious about God and discover more from his word, and as we connect with others giving and receiving the love which comes from God himself. Notice how Peter speaks of making an *"effort"*. This is about dedication, something in our hearts which longs to grow more like Jesus, something which God never wants us to lose. As we grow these qualities, as the goodness of God more and more takes over our lives, the effects will be observable by those around us.

The Christians in Thessalonica had this desire. Paul wrote to them and said, *"Your faith in God has become known everywhere"* (1 Thessalonians 1:8). He went on to tell them that what others had seen was how they had *"turned from idols to serve the true and living God"* (1 Thessalonians 1:9). Their faith had become their way of life, observable in their habits and their attitudes. These things cannot be quantified, but they can be seen. Paul reached a time in his life when he knew that he was about to die. He said this to his young friend Timothy, *"For I am already being poured out like a drink offering, and the time for my departure is near. I have fought the good fight, I have finished the race, I have kept the faith"* (2 Timothy 4:6-7). For Paul the most important thing was that he had *"kept the faith".* At the end of the day, for each one of us that is the issue: not whether we have grown church, but whether we have grown faith, kept the faith and kept the faith *growing* through all the challenges of our lives.

Jesus said that *"by their fruit you will recognise them"* (Matthew 7:20). Paul uses the same idea when he speaks of the fruit of the Spirit: *"the fruit of the Spirit is love, joy, peace, forbearance, kindness, goodness, faithfulness, gentleness and self-control* (Galatians 5:22-23). Recently I heard the testimony of a man from Iran who was brought up a very devout Muslim and is now a Christian leading a number of churches in the Middle East. The process of his conversion was slow, and came with a lot of soul searching and questioning. But the pivotal moment for him came when he read the words of Jesus about fruit, and he looked at the Christian community he had been observing, comparing it to the religion with which he had been brought up. He said that *"as soon as I looked at them like that I knew where I belonged."* The fruit of love and kindness, of forgiveness and acceptance, of grace and goodness was overwhelming for him, and drew him to Jesus.

This underlines for me the whole message of this book. As we grow in our faith, there will be a witness in our lives to the work of the Spirit in us; "the fullness of Christ" will be on display and others will be drawn to believe in Jesus. Our key focus needs to be growing faith which will in turn lead to a growing church.

Conclusion

One of my favourite radio programmes has to be *"Gardeners Question Time"*. It was first broadcast in the Northern region of the BBC Home service at 22.15 on 9 April 1947, over 79 years ago! It came from the Smallshaw Allotments Association and the programme title was initially, *"How Does your Garden Grow?"* My grandmother used to listen to it every week. You would have thought after a few years they would have given all the instructions necessary for good gardening! But no, gardening is not mechanical, it is organic, and it keeps on changing. So even today there is more to find out, and *"Gardeners Question Time"* continues! Some of the panellists over the years have become household names, but they have never tried to tell people exactly how to garden. It is always a matter of suggestion. I love the suggestion that one of my gardening heroes, Monty Don, offers in his book *"Fork to Fork"*. [67] Talking about the time to sow seeds he suggests we look out for the arrival of weed seedlings in the ground Here there are no specific dates or

[67] Don, M. (2010). *Fork to Fork*. Octopus Books

instructions, just good suggestions! In its own way that suggestion applies to our faith: when is a good time to growth more faith? When the challenges of life are beginning to show through the surface. My suggestion is that if we dedicate ourselves to the three areas of conversation, curiosity and connections, we will be doing our part to keep our faith growing. Paul said, *"We are servants through whom you came to believe"* (1 Corinthians 3:5). As we do so, it is the Spirit of God who will make our faith grow. He will increase our taste for the goodness of God and this will affect our lives in ways that others will notice; there will be fruit on display.

So to end, here are some simple questions which may well help you and me to keep faith growing.

When did I last converse with God, not just to tell him all about my problems and my longings and prayers for others, but actually listen to him and hear his voice as I read the Bible, as I look around me and as I am still in his presence? Pray: "Lord grow in me the faith that is aware of you here and now, and trusts in your goodness and love whatever is going on."

What have I recently discovered about the Lord? When did I last get excited about finding something new in the Bible, or realise something new from the Spirit as I wonder about this world? When did I last experience some revelation about this amazing creation God has given me, or hear good news of Jesus at work in someone's life? Pray: "Lord, grow in me a curiosity for more of you. Forgive me for settling for what I think I know when you have so much more to show me. And Lord, help me to let the difficulties in life become opportunities to trust you more deeply."

Who, in all the people I mingle with has reminded me recently that everyone is precious to God, and everyone matters to me? Am I conscious of the importance of the connections God has given me with his family? Am I seeking to strengthen those connections? And am I seeking to connect with those around me who do not yet share faith in Jesus? Pray: "Lord to know you and love you is so good, and to have connections with others because of you makes life so rich. Help me to grow these connections for your glory."

Pray: "Lord increase I pray my taste for your goodness! May my trust in you be strong and my desire to be a display of your glory to others, for Jesus sake. Lord, make me more like Jesus."

Paul wrote to the Christians at Philippi and told them that the reason why God had spared him to continue working among them was *"for your progress and joy in the faith"* (Philippians 1:25). I hope these words will in some small way contribute to that as well. May God work in all of us to bring progress and joy in our faith.

Bibliography

Bolz-Weber, N. (2013) *Cranky Beautiful Faith*, Canterbury Press

Bonhoeffer, D. (1937), *The Cost of Discipleship.* Pocket Books; 1st Touchstone Ed edition, 1995

Duffet, Chris. (2009). *Smack Heads and Fat Cats.* Gilead Books Publishing

Duffet, Chris & Goddard, Simon. (2012). *Big Hearted.* Gilead Books Publishing

Fee, G. (1994), *God's Empowering Presence.* Baker Publishing

Ffrench-Beytagh, G, (1975). *Encountering Light.* Fontana

Grylls, B. (2011), *Mud sweat and tears.* Transworld Publishers, London

Keller, T. (2013), *Encounters with Jesus*, Hodder & Stoughton

Lawrence, B. (1693), *The Practice of the Presence of God.* Wilder Publications 2008

Lucado, M. (2012), *He chose the nails.* Nelson

Lucado, M. (2000), *You are Special.* Crossway

Nouwen, H. (1981), *The Genesee Diary*. Darton, Longman & Todd

Peterson, E. (2006), *Living The Resurrection*. Navpress

Piper, J. (2002/2013), *Brothers we are not professionals*. Broadman & Holman Publishers, Nashville, Tennessee

Polkinghorne, J. (2005), *Exploring Reality*. SPCK

Ponsonby, S. (2004), *More*. David C. Cook

Schuller, R. H. (1991) *Life's not fair but God is good*. Bantam

Simpson, B. (2012), *When butterflies speak*. Xlibris

Yakonelli, M. (2001), *Messy Spirituality*. Hodder and Stoughton